softies

softies

22 friends for you to sew, knit and crochet

VIKING
an imprint of
PENGUIN BOOKS

contents

introduction 1

before you start 2

mibala 4

lucy's monster 14

polly 18

bunny 24

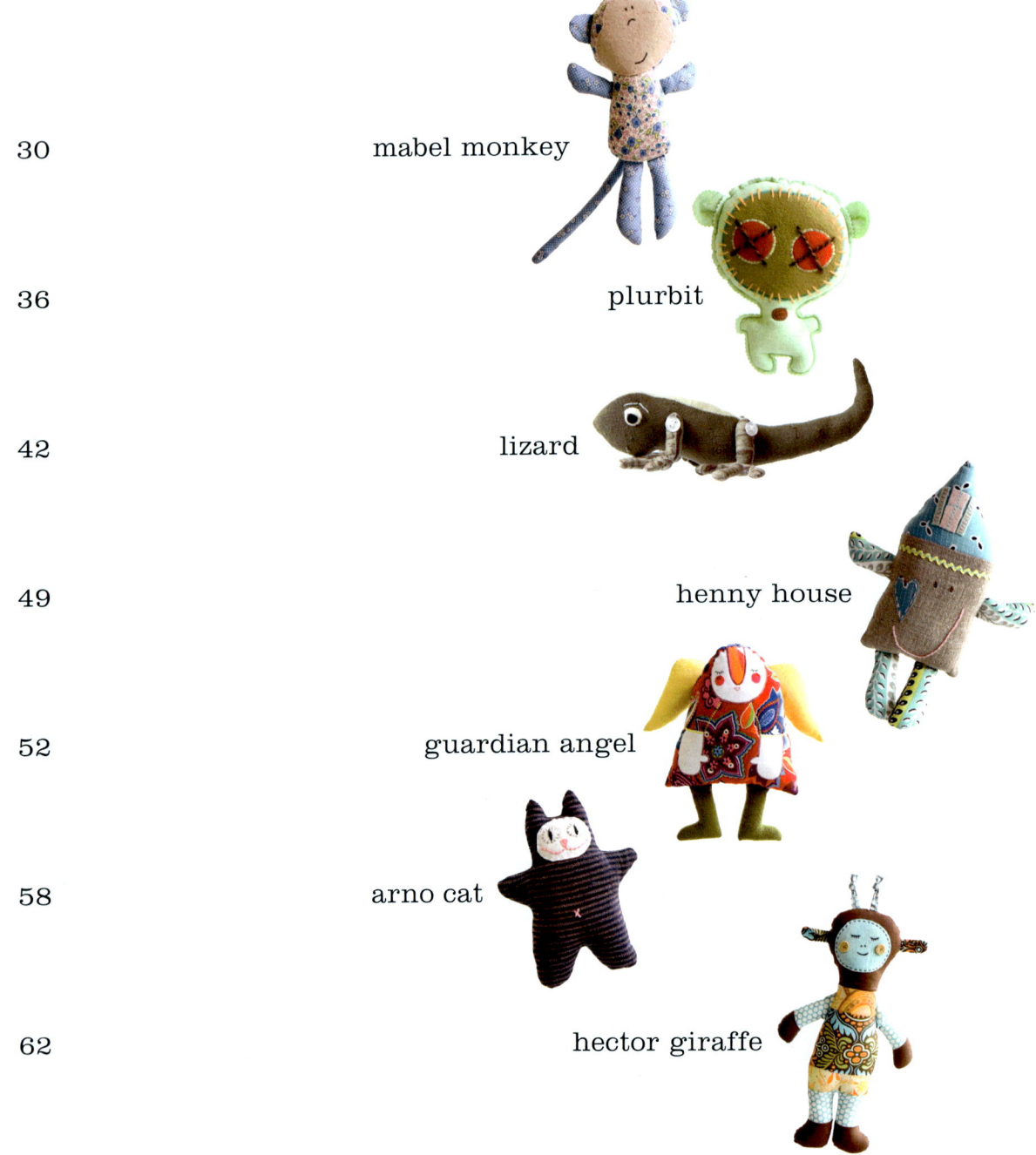

30 mabel monkey

36 plurbit

42 lizard

49 henny house

52 guardian angel

58 arno cat

62 hector giraffe

mamma bear 68

kangaroo 74

blossom bunny 80

pirate 86

beetle bug 99

cat 104

mad dog 108

112 cosmonaut devil

118 donkey

124 albert monkey

132 owl

139 glossary

143 fabric credits

introduction

Home-made designer soft toys are all the rage. All you have to do is type 'softies' into an internet search engine, and you'll find yourself knee-deep in the blogs of thousands of crafters and artists sharing and selling their inspiring creations online.

For this book, we've sourced contributors from around the world. Included are instructions and patterns for original and charming soft toys that will appeal to adults and children alike — because softies are definitely not just for the kids anymore.

The toys are made using a range of techniques, from simple hand-sewing to knitting and crochet, and each one is completely individual and unique. Each entry includes a list of tools and materials that you'll need, as well as detailed instructions, hints and tips.

Making your own soft toys gives you the opportunity to nourish the child within, to be creative and take time out from all the grown-up concerns of hectic everyday life. And the result of your work is a hand-made gift that has been stitched with love and care — a personal touch that's impossible to buy.

before you start

Before you start, there are a few basic things to note:

- Pre-wash and iron all fabrics before beginning.

- All patterns include a 6 mm (¼ in) seam allowance. However, note that felt pieces such as noses and eyes will not have seam allowances, as they don't require them.

- Each pattern specifies how much to enlarge it, in order to make the toy at the size pictured. However, you can enlarge the patterns to whatever size you desire – just remember that your fabric requirements will change.

- When tracing pattern pieces onto tracing paper, be sure to transfer all markings.

- Any toys with small parts such as buttons are not suitable for children under three years of age. However, in most instances these components could be substituted with felt, fabric or embroidery.

- The glossary at the back of the book is a quick, handy reference that includes definitions of commonly used terms and abbreviations, as well as explanations of how to do basic sewing, knitting and crochet stitches.

- Instructions for some of the toys will direct you to pin the pre-sewn arms, legs and/or ears into place on the right side of one body piece, 'pointing in towards the body'. This is so that when you sew the two body pieces together (right sides facing), you will attach the limbs/ears to the body at the same time. It is important to ensure you position the appendages so that they will be facing the right way when the toy is turned right side out (e.g. so that the toes point outwards). The diagram below shows an example of how to pin limbs onto the body correctly. It shows one body piece placed right side up, with limbs pinned on (pointing in towards the body). The next step would be to place the remaining body piece right side down on top, and sew around the body (leaving an opening for turning right side out and stuffing).

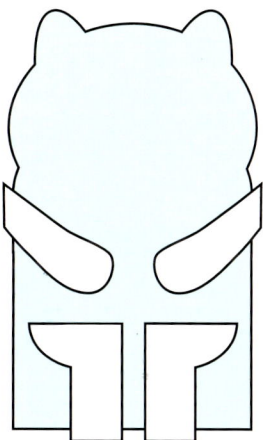

mibala

{Soozs – www.soozs.blogspot.com} SUZIE FRY

Mibala is a large stuffed toy made from felted wool. Felt materials have a lovely fuzzy feel to them, and just look better as they age – this is a toy that will stand up to many cuddles and years of play. You can recycle old materials (like an old woollen jumper or blanket) to make Mibala, so it's an economical toy to make. It is also not a difficult doll to make, but you will require a little patience to get the limbs attached securely and the face looking good. Don't be afraid to experiment with the finer details and the materials you use – every toy should have its own personality and unique features.

FINISHED SIZE
27 cm × 19 cm (10½ in × 7½ in) – body only

TOOLS
- Tracing paper
- Scissors
- Pins
- Sewing needle
- Sewing machine
- Stuffing stick (or chopstick or pencil)
- Iron
- Washing machine

MATERIALS
- Body fabric – a woollen blanket or woollen jumper (must be 100 per cent pure wool). Using a blanket will result in a much stiffer result, more like a traditional stuffed doll, whereas the knitted jumper version will be softer and more huggable.
- Extra fabric – small pieces of felt for the mouth, eyes, heart and belly button, in contrasting colours.
- Thread – coloured sewing thread to match the body felt.
- Stuffing – preferably use wool rovings because they are a natural fibre and wear well, but you can substitute polyfill if you don't have wool.

(CONTINUED)

{mibala}

INSTRUCTIONS

1 Begin by felting (fulling) your woollen blanket or jumper. I find the easiest way to felt a woollen item is to use the washing machine. First, make sure your blanket or jumper is 100 per cent pure wool and is not labelled 'machine washable', as artificial fibres and certain wool treatments will prevent felting. Put your item in a hot wash/cold rinse cycle with a mild detergent.

Felting is a gradual process, and you can therefore choose the degree to which you want to felt: the longer the wash, the more the item will shrink, and the denser and stiffer the final fabric will be. If you find at the end of the wash that the fabric hasn't felted enough, simply repeat the wash cycle. However, be aware that very dense fabrics are harder to sew – especially when you have to sew through multiple layers of fabric at once, such as where the limbs join the body.

If using a woollen jumper for this project, I felt just enough to stop the fabric fraying when cut, as this results in a finished toy that has a bit more stretch and squish.

The degree of stretch in the felted wool will affect the final shape of your toy, as will the orientation of the stretch. For example, if you have the stretch going horizontally from side to side (like a conventional piece of stretch clothing), your Mibala will be wider and squatter that if you have the stretch going vertically up and down.

Always dry your felt flat; you may need to pull the item into shape while still damp. Iron well when dry (on the wrong side of the felt, on a wool setting), to ensure the fabric is smooth and even.

2 Trace and cut out the enlarged pattern using the template provided. Pin it to the felt and cut out the pieces. You will need to cut 2 body shapes, 4 arm shapes, 4 leg shapes, 4 horn shapes, 1 mouth shape and 2 eye shapes from your fabric. You may also like to cut out a little felt heart and use a knot of felt for a belly button. If you are using a felted jumper make sure you match the direction of the stretch for all the pieces.

If the jumper has any interesting detailing, you might want to use it to add extra definition to the pattern. For example, a ribbed band might be used to highlight the difference between the hand and arm.

{mibala}

3 For each of the arms, legs and horns, pin 2 pieces together (right sides facing), and sew with the sewing machine, leaving a small opening on one side of each arm and leg for turning right side out and stuffing (as marked on the pattern). Leave the base of the horns open for turning right side out (they won't be stuffed). If your felt has stretch, make sure you use a stretch stitch on your machine or the stitches will break when the toy is stretched. After sewing, clip all curves close to the seam to allow for a smoother finish after turning right side out. Turn all pieces right side out and press flat with the iron.

4 Sew face details onto one of the body shapes. I use a straight stretch stitch on the sewing machine, but you can use a more conventional zigzag appliqué style, or sew by hand. Hand sew on the heart and belly button (as marked) if using.

5 Place this body piece right side up on your work surface. Pin the limbs and horns in position (x to x, y to y, and z to z) pointing in towards the body and remembering which way they will face when the body is turned right side out (see diagram on page 3).

Make sure the stuffing openings in the limbs are on the underside of the arms and the insides of the legs (so they show the least). Place the second body piece right side down on top and pin the two body pieces together. Sew, remembering to leave an opening on one side for turning right side out and stuffing (as marked). After sewing, clip all curves close to the seam. Turn right side out.

6 Using a stuffing stick, stuff each limb using small pieces of stuffing. Try to stuff all limbs evenly. Remember that stuffing compacts over time, and if you are using a stiffer blanket felt you will want the stuffing to be firmer or the toy will soon become lumpy. Sew each stuffing opening closed using a whip stitch.

7 Stuff the main body, taking care to push stuffing well into the head and corners. Sew the stuffing opening closed using a whip stitch.

8 You can clothe Mibala in a cotton sundress or a simple wrap dress made of felt (see instructions on page 8).

(CONTINUED)

{mibala}

Sundress

MATERIALS
- Fabric – two pieces of lightweight patterned cotton, each measuring 25 cm × 30 cm (10 in × 12 in).
- Thread – coloured sewing thread to match fabric.
- Decorations – a 60 cm (24 in) length of fine ribbon or cord.

INSTRUCTIONS

1 Start by checking the sundress pattern dimensions against your finished doll. This is important because felted jumpers and blankets will vary in thickness and stretch so your finished doll may end up slightly taller or wider than mine. If so, adjust the pattern to fit.

2 Trace and cut out the enlarged pattern using the template provided. Pin it to the fabric and cut out the pieces. You will need to cut 2 sundress shapes from your fabric.

3 Use a zigzag stitch to sew all around the edge of each dress piece to prevent fraying.

4 Pin dress pieces together (right sides facing) and sew side seams from the bottom hem to the underarm opening (as marked on the pattern). Iron the side seams open right up to the neck edge.

5 Hem the upper side seams – don't sew them together, as this will form the arm opening. Iron seams and then sew a hem around the bottom of the dress.

6 Sew a hem around the neck, making sure the hem is wide enough to accommodate your chosen ribbon or cord. Thread the ribbon or cord through both neck edges and tie to one side.

Wrap dress

MATERIALS
- Fabric – a piece of wool felt measuring 25 cm × 55 cm (10 in × 22 in). I prefer to use store-bought craft felt because I like the finish and weight, but you could use a felted blanket or jumper if you prefer.
- Thread – coloured sewing thread to match felt.
- Decorations – small pieces of felt in contrasting colours, or embroidery thread; 1 small button.

INSTRUCTIONS

1 Start by checking the coat-dress pattern dimensions against your finished doll. This is important because

{mibala}

felted jumpers and blankets will vary in thickness and stretch so your finished doll may end up slightly taller or wider than mine. If so, adjust the pattern to fit.

2 Trace and cut out the enlarged pattern using the template provided. Pin it to the felt and cut out the piece. You will need to cut 1 coat-dress shape from your felt.

3 Cut a button hole on the outside flap (as marked on the pattern), and finish using a blanket stitch.

4 Sew button onto inside flap (as marked on the pattern).

5 Sew a decorative felt motif or embroider detail onto the outer coat flap if you desire.

Enlarge template to 150% Seam allowance is included

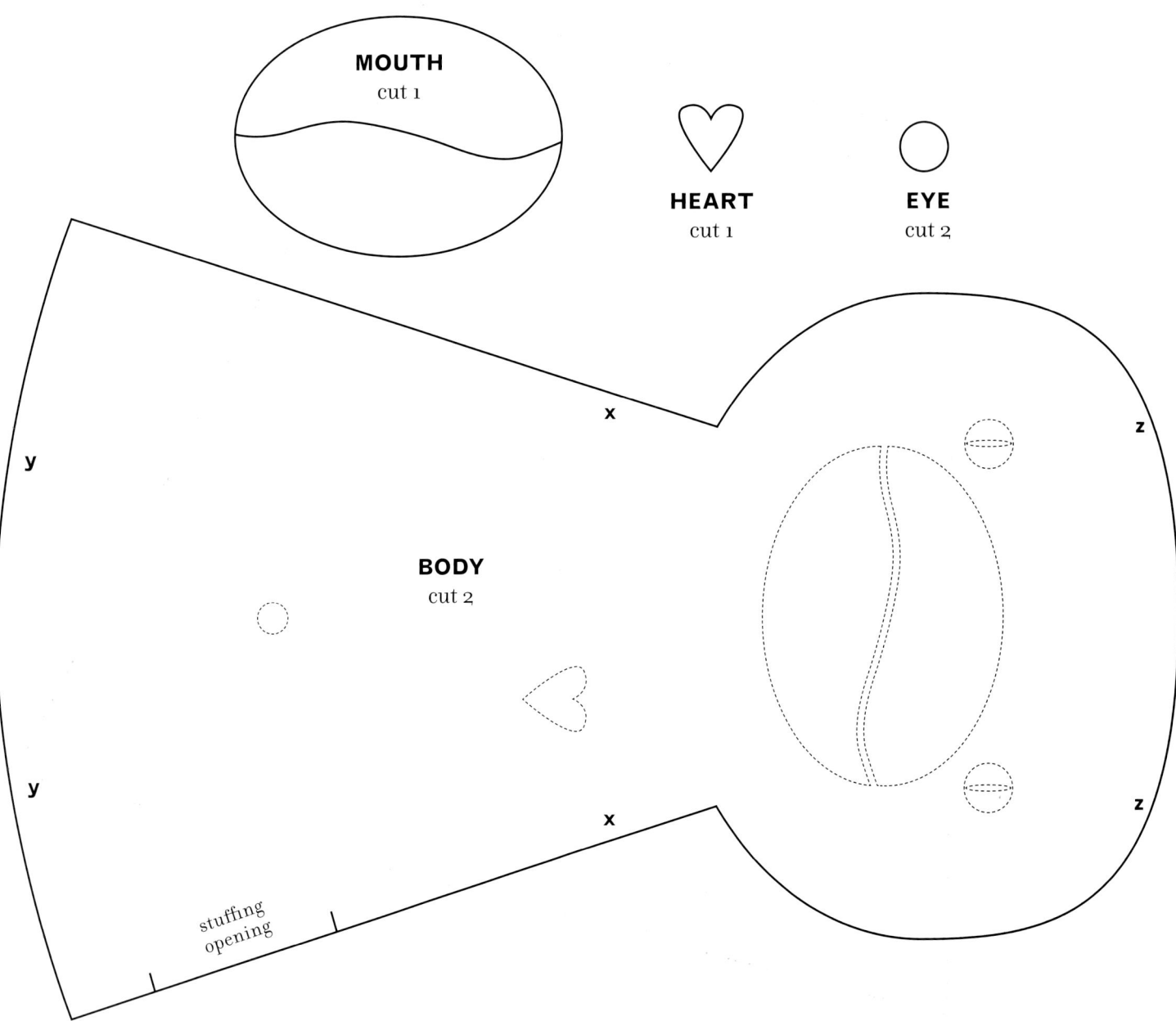

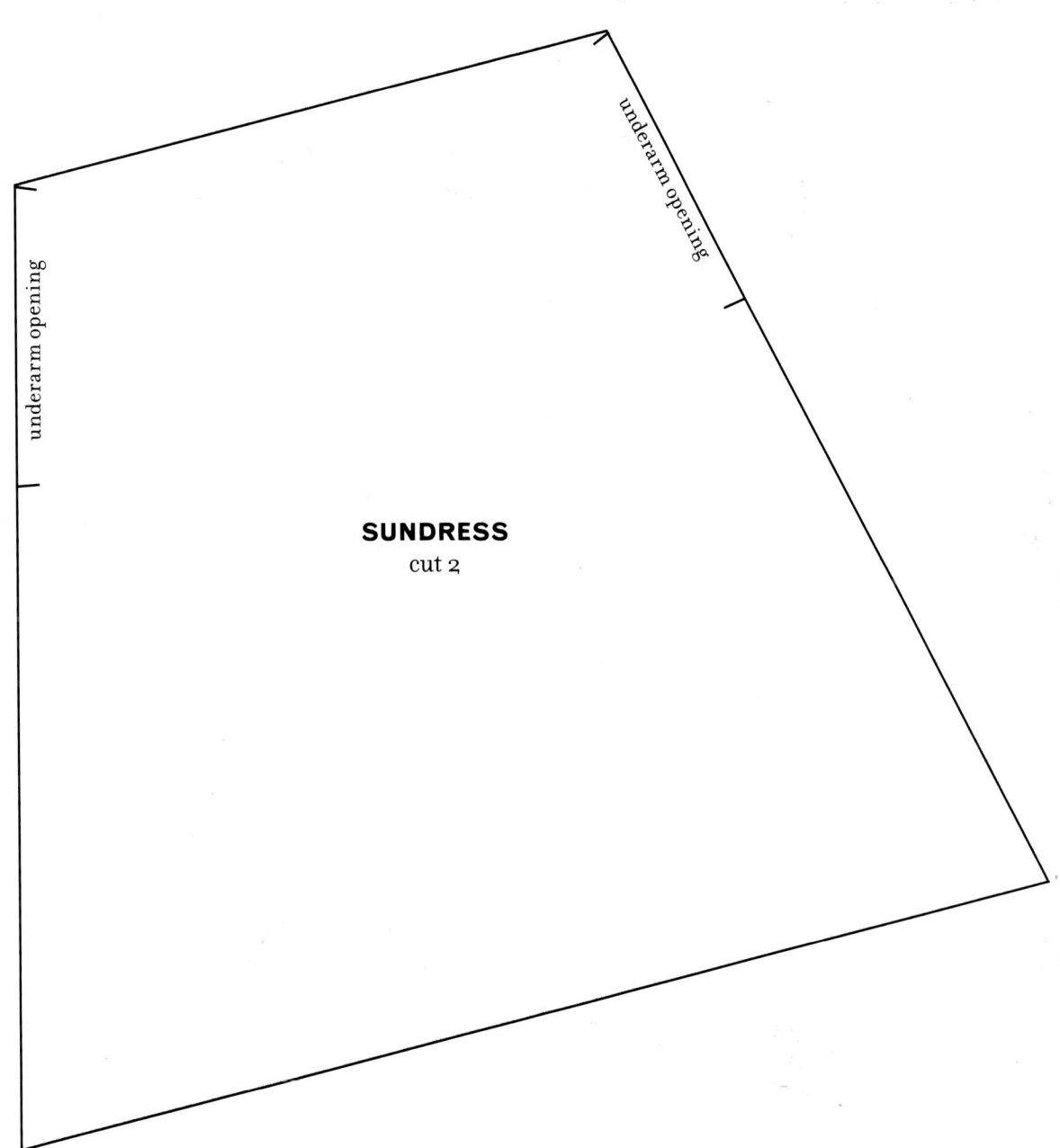

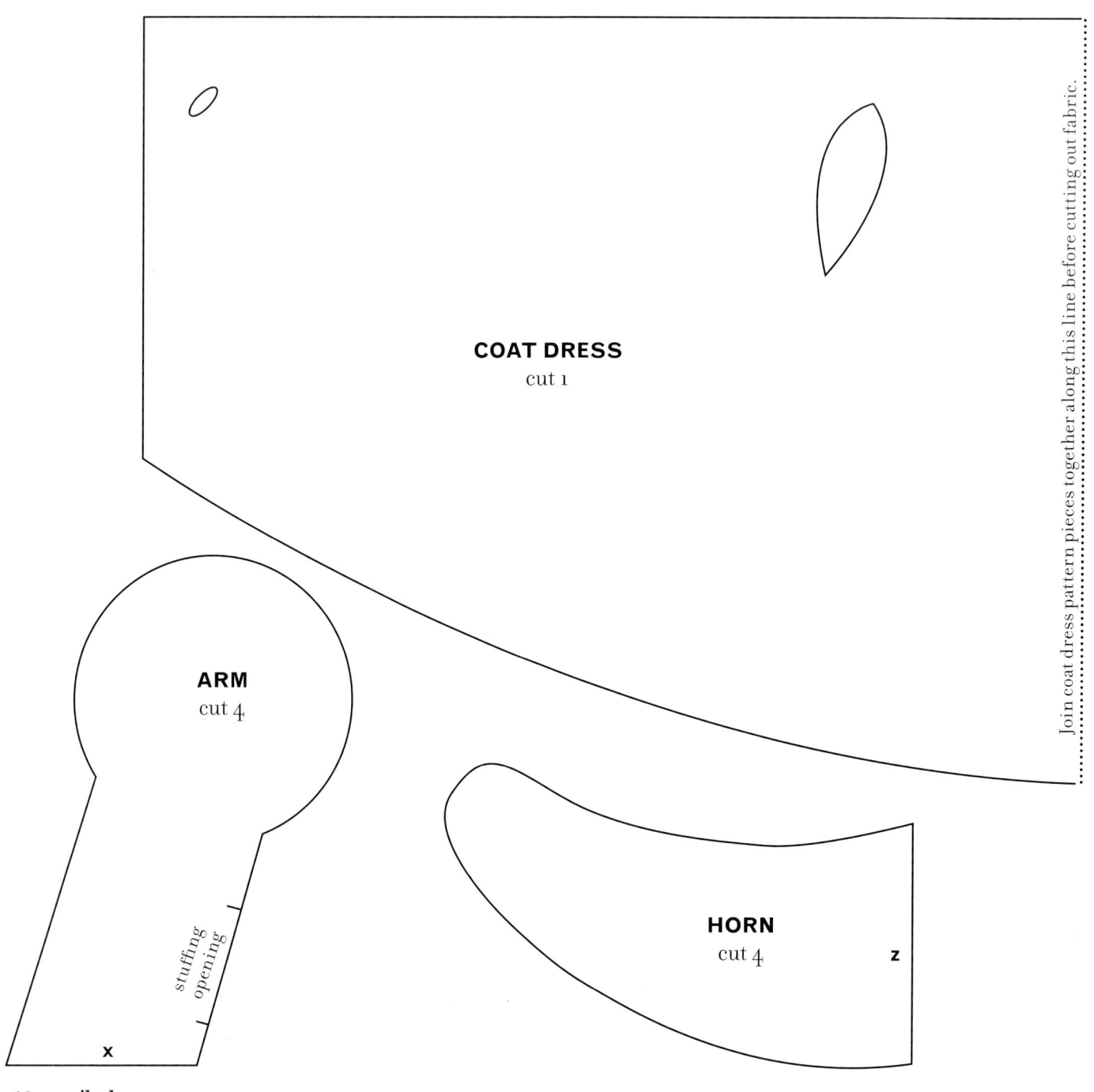

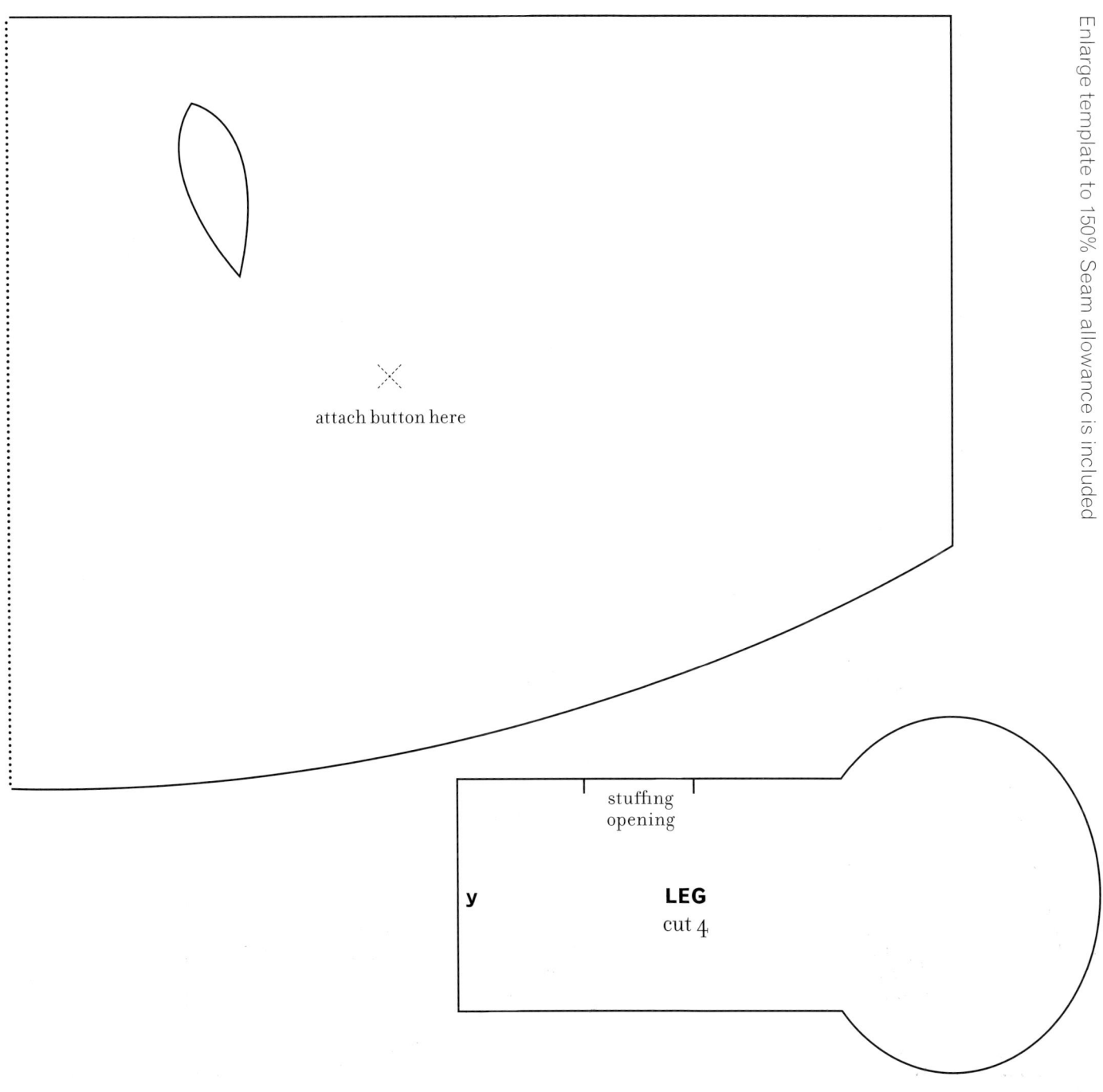

Lucy's monster

{heylucy.typepad.com} MARNÉ CALES

This little monster appeals to kids because of its simple, vibrant nature. Using safety eyes means it's appropriate for all ages, and the wool felt makes it easily washable.

FINISHED SIZE
22 cm × 18 cm (8½ in × 7 in)

TOOLS
- Tracing paper
- Scissors
- Pins
- Sewing needle
- Sewing machine
- Stuffing stick (or chopstick or pencil)

MATERIALS
- Body fabric – a 46 cm × 40 cm (17 in × 16 in) piece of wool felt or wool-blend felt.
- Extra fabric – scraps of white felt for the eyes.
- Thread – black or dark-brown embroidery thread for the eyes and mouth. Dental floss for attaching the eyes.
- Decorations – two 10–12 mm (2/5 in) safety eyes (for children under 3 years) or two small 12 mm (2/5 in) buttons (for children over 3 years).
- Stuffing – polyfill or wool rovings.

INSTRUCTIONS

1 The method for sewing Lucy's monster is different to the other sewing patterns in this book; the body pieces are not cut out of the fabric until after you have sewn the pieces together. This is to make sewing around the tight curves easier.

2 First, trace and cut out the enlarged pattern pieces using the template provided. You will need 2 body pattern pieces and 2 eye pattern pieces. Pin the pattern pieces to the felt and trace around them using a fabric marker. Carefully mark the position of the eyes and mouth. Do not cut the body fabric yet. Cut out the 2 eye pieces from the white felt.

3 Using the embroidery thread, blanket stitch the felt eye pieces into place. Then sew a mouth using a stem stitch. Attach the safety eyes or buttons to the centre of the felt eye pieces – I find that sewing them on with

{CONTINUED}

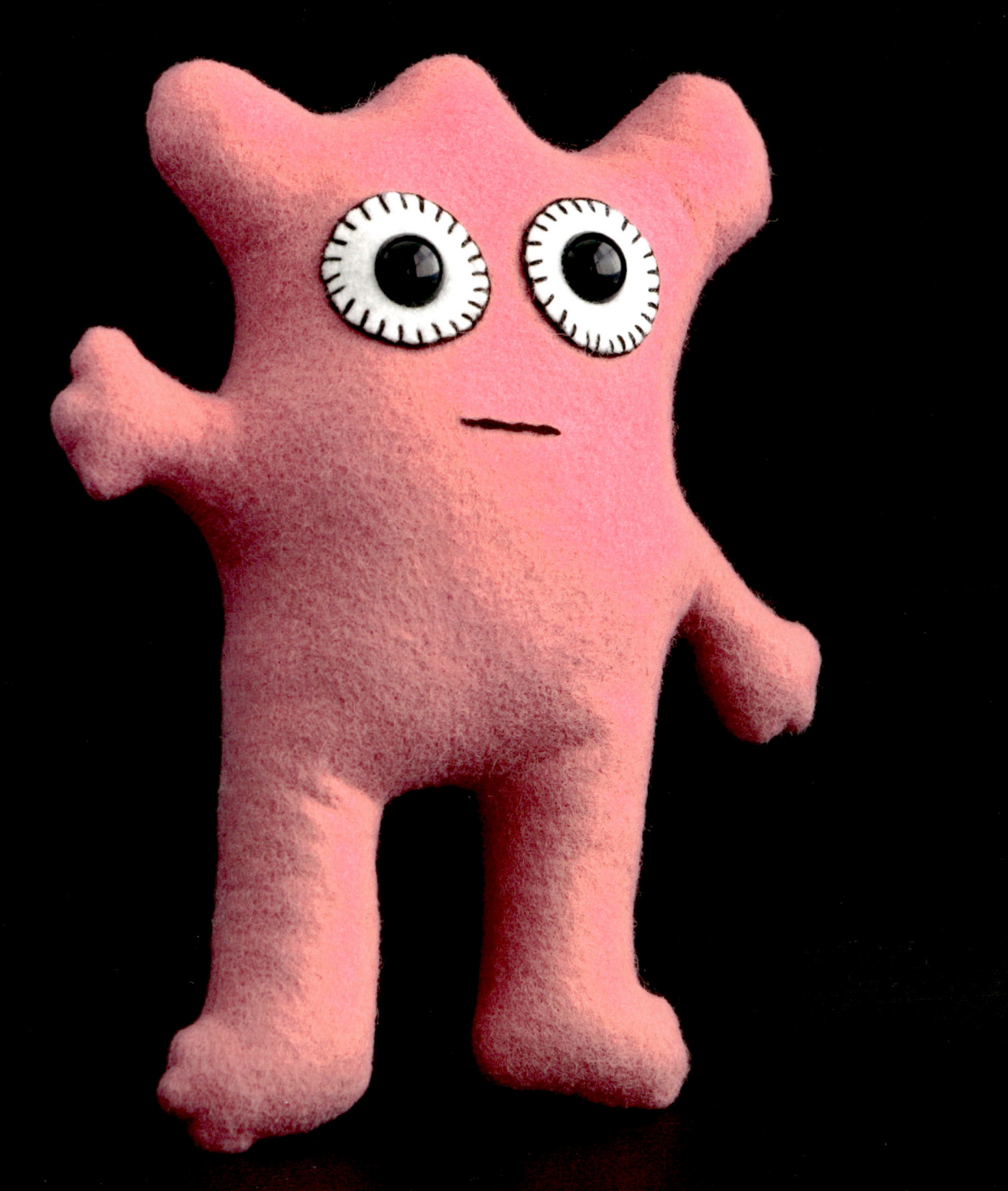

{lucy's monster}

dental floss makes them much more likely to stay in place.

4 Pin body pieces together (right sides facing), taking care to ensure you have lined up the pieces correctly. Set your sewing machine to a short straight stitch – this makes going around all those tight curves and corners much easier, and will make your seams sturdier. Sew all around the body, pivoting with the needle at each corner. Leave an opening for turning right side out and stuffing, as marked on the pattern.

5 Now you can cut out the body shape. Use the stitching as a guide, but leave at least a 10 mm (⅜ in) border. Working with one layer of the seam allowance at a time, use scissors to clip all the inside curves and notch all the outside curves. (Be careful not to clip the seam.) Stagger the nicks and notches on the two layers of the seam allowance, as this will ensure the seams are strong and lie smooth. Turn right side out.

6 Using a stuffing stick, push small amounts of stuffing into the tight corners first –toes, fingers, arms, legs and head lumps. Gradually fill the rest of the body until the stuffing is firm and even.

7 Sew the stuffing opening closed using a slip stitch.

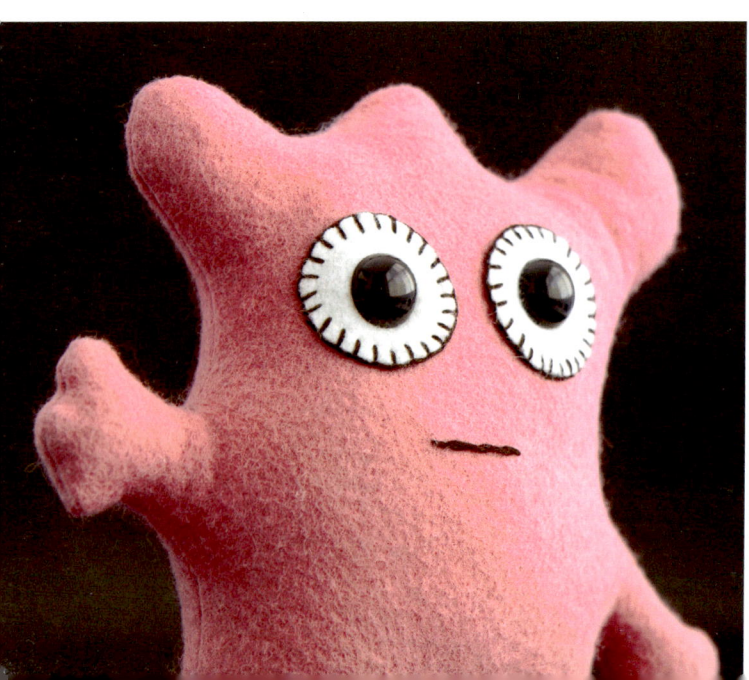

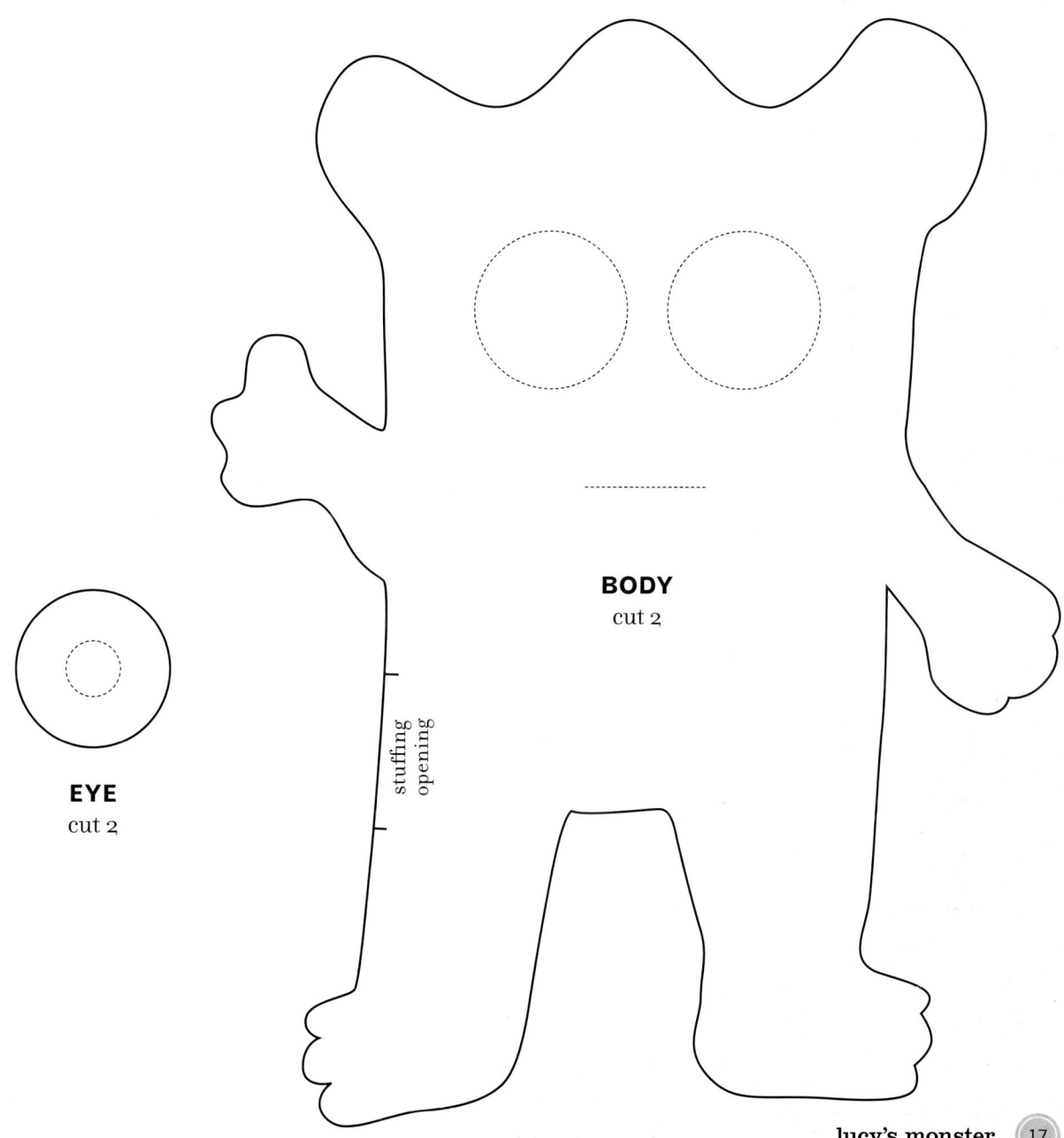

polly

{Nest Studio – neststudio.typepad.com} CARLY SCHWERDT

With her sunny smile and fun combination of retro fabrics, Polly makes a charming friend.

FINISHED SIZE
21 cm × 17 cm (8 in × 6½ in) – body only

TOOLS
Tracing paper
Scissors
Pins
Sewing needle
Sewing machine
Stuffing stick (or chopstick or pencil)

MATERIALS
- Body fabric – a 14 cm × 40 cm (5½ in × 16 in) piece of quality cotton fabric for the body.
- Extra fabric – scraps of cotton fabric in complementary colours for the arms and ears, scraps of striped fabric for the legs; a fat quarter of wool blanketing for the head; a 14 cm × 9 cm (5½ in × 3½ in) piece wool felt in beige, cream or brown for the face; scraps of felt for the hair.
- Thread – coloured sewing thread to match fabric, plus black and red sewing thread for the face details.
- Stuffing – polyfill or wool rovings.

(CONTINUED)

{polly}

INSTRUCTIONS

1 Trace and cut out the enlarged pattern using the template provided. Pin it to the appropriate fabric and cut out the pieces. (I like to cut freehand without a pattern, as it makes for individual quirky toys – you can try this, using the pattern as a rough guide). You will need to cut 2 body shapes, 4 leg shapes, 4 arm shapes, 4 ear shapes, 1 face shape, 2 head shapes and 1 hair shape from your fabric.

2 For each leg, pin pieces together (right sides facing) and sew together with the sewing machine, leaving a small opening as indicated on the pattern for turning right side out and stuffing. Repeat for arms and ears. (There's no need to leave a stuffing opening for the ears, as they will not be stuffed, but leave the base open for turning right side out.) Turn each piece right side out.

3 For the face, use the sewing thread to neatly sew felt face piece to one of the woollen head pieces. Sew on felt hair and embroider nose, mouth and eyes with sewing thread (as shown on the pattern).

{polly}

4 Pin each head piece to a body piece (right sides facing) and sew.

5 Place one head/body piece right side up on your work surface. Pin the ears, arms and legs into place (x to x, y to y and z to z), pointing in towards the body and remembering which way they will face when the body is turned right side out (see diagram on page 3). Make sure the stuffing openings in the limbs end up on the underside of the arms and the inside of the legs (so they show the least). Place the second body piece right side down on top and pin the two pieces together. Sew all around the body and head, securing the limbs and ears in place as you go, and leaving a 4 cm (1½ in) opening under one arm for turning right side out and stuffing (as marked). (I always double stitch over the arms and legs, to make them extra strong.)

6 Trim all edges, but leave at least a 10 mm (⅖ in) border. With scissors, clip fabric around the curves. Be careful not to clip the seam. Turn right side out (take your time, as this can be a bit tricky).

7 Using a stuffing stick, push small amounts of stuffing into each of the limbs, then sew openings closed using a whip stitch. Gradually fill the rest of the body until the stuffing is firm and even, but not too tight.

8 Sew the stuffing opening closed using a whip stitch.

{CONTINUED}

Enlarge template to 130% Seam allowance is included

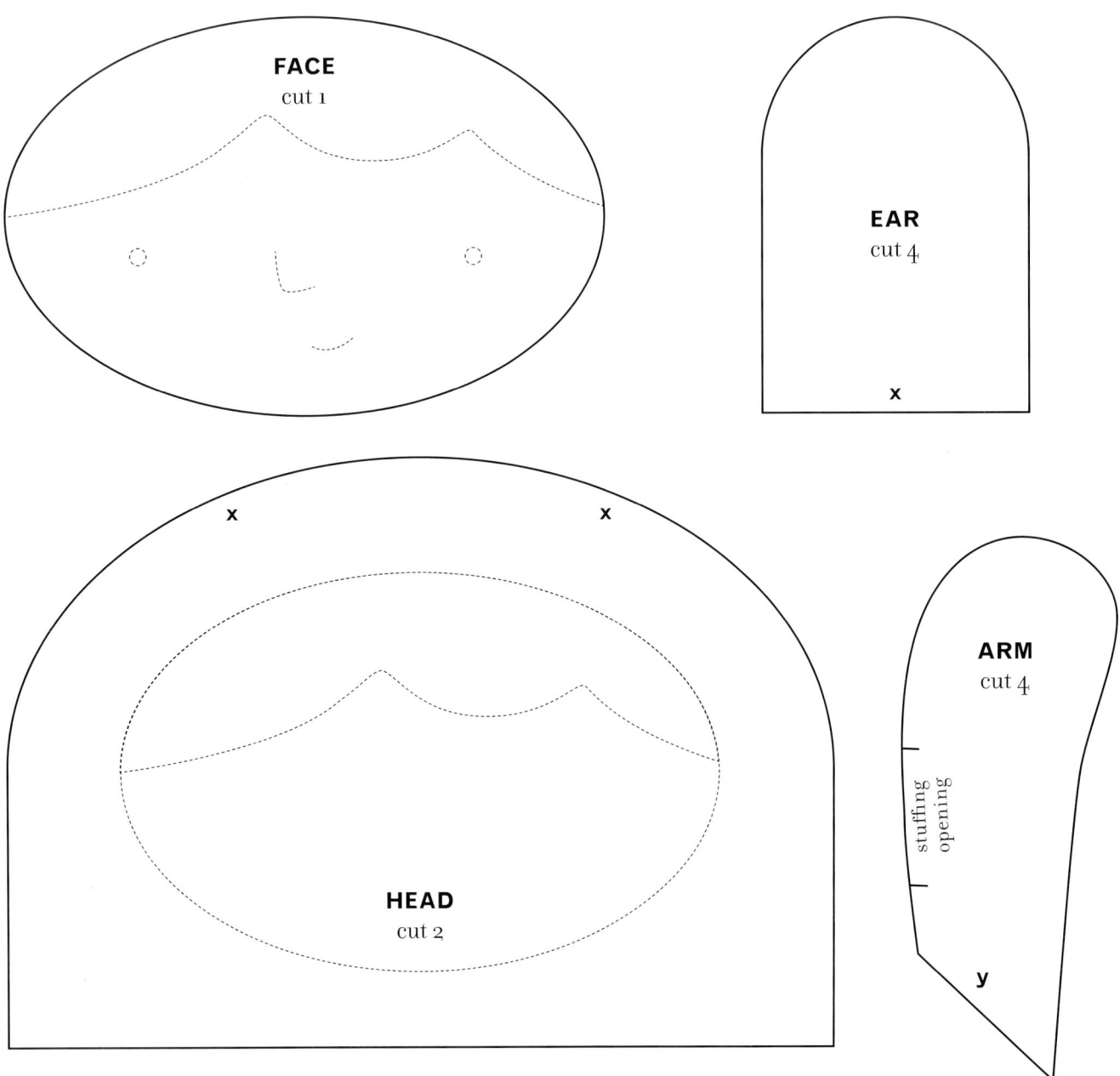

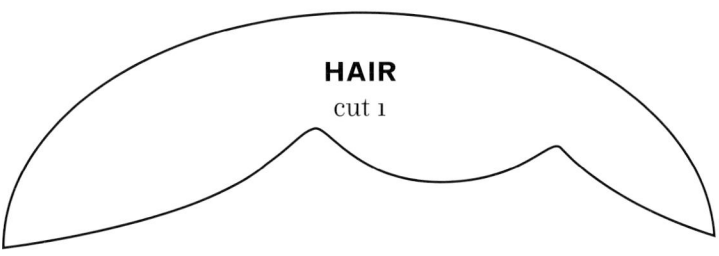

HAIR
cut 1

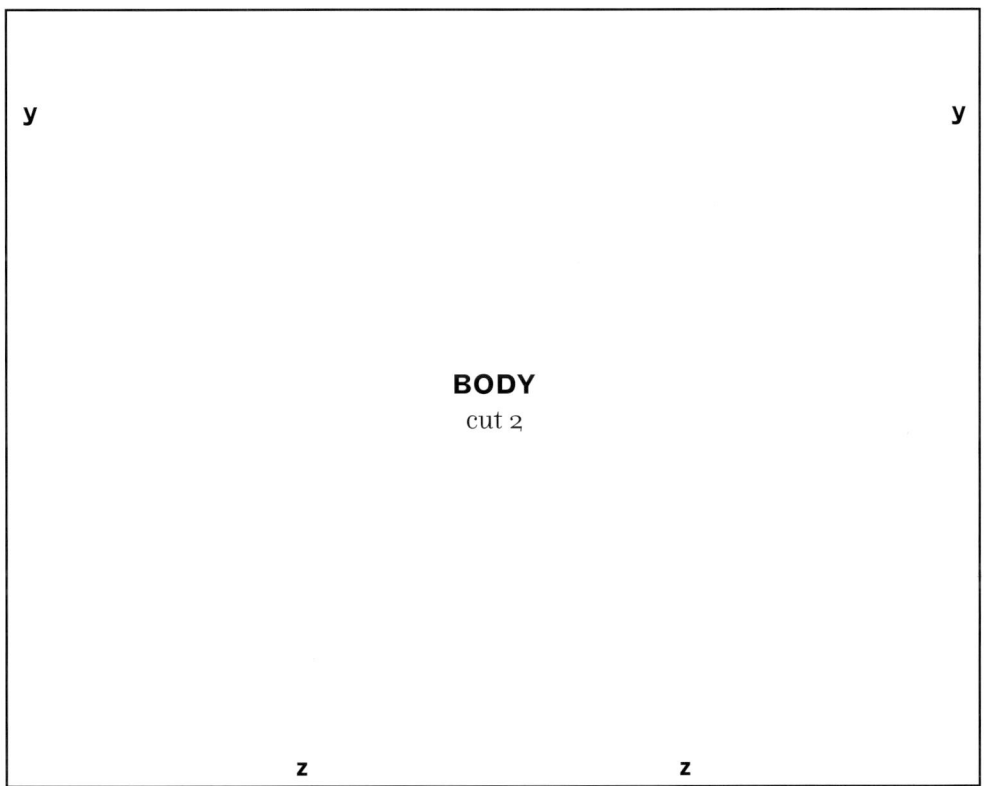

y　　　　　　　　　　　　　　　　y

BODY
cut 2

z　　　　z

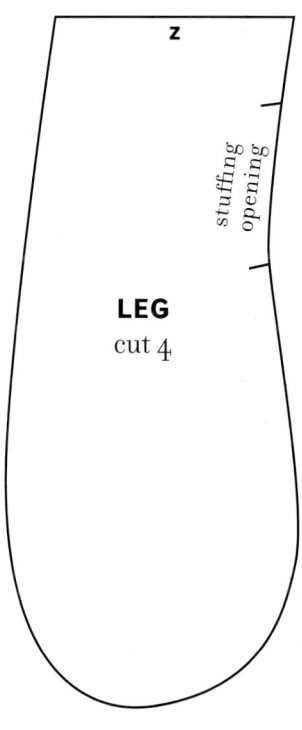

z

stuffing opening

LEG
cut 4

polly

bunny

{karkovski — www.karkovski.typepad.com} KRISTINA KARKOV THERKILDSEN

This bunny emerged when I was practising knitting with four needles. I was originally planning to knit a little girl doll, but halfway through my doll turned into a rabbit! These instructions explain how to knit the bunny either with four regular knitting needles, or with a circular needle.

FINISHED SIZE
15 cm × 8 cm (6 in × 3 in) – body only

TOOLS
- 4 × 2.5 mm (US size 1/UK size 13) knitting needles or 1 × 2.5 mm, 20 cm (8 in) circular double-pointed needle
- Tracing paper
- Scissors
- Pins
- Sewing needle and/or machine
- Stuffing stick (or chopstick or pencil)

MATERIALS
- Fabric – scraps of coloured felt or fabric for the feet, arms and ears, plus another piece for the heart (this can be the same or contrasting).
- Extra fabric – a small piece of white felt or fabric for the snout, plus any scrap of fabric for the rice bag.
- Yarn – two balls 4-ply cotton yarn: 1 ball pink (MC) and 1 ball white (CC).
- Decorations – two matching buttons for eyes. 1 different button for the nose. (You may want to try out different colours and sizes before you attach them.) A small white pompom for the tail.
- Thread – white sewing thread. Embroidery thread to match button colours.
- Stuffing – polyfill and rice.

(CONTINUED)

{bunny}

INSTRUCTIONS

1 Begin by knitting the body. If using 4 needles, cast on 60 stitches evenly across 3 needles. If using a circular needle, place a marker before the first stitch (so that you can keep count of the number of rounds knitted). Then, using knit stitch, knit:

    MC 5 rounds
    CC 3 rounds
    MC 3 rounds
    CC 3 rounds

Continue this pattern until you have 16 stripes, or about 10 cm (4 in). If using a circular needle, place 2 more markers – 1 at the 20th stitch and one at the 40th. Then, using knit stitch, knit:

    MC 3 rounds

Continue using the MC and decrease by one stitch at the beginning of each needle (or at each marker if using a circular needle) until you have only 6 stitches left on each needle (or 18 for circular needle). (Decrease by knitting 2 stitches together through the front of the stitches.) Break yarn off, leaving a 20 cm (8 in) tail. Thread the tail through the remaining stitches and secure. Secure the rest of the threads and cut off. At this stage you should have a tube shape that is closed at one end.

2 Using a stuffing stick, stuff the body firmly.

3 For the fabric pieces, trace and cut out the enlarged pattern using the template provided. Pin it to the felt or fabric and cut out the pieces. You will need to cut out 2 leg shapes (cut on the fold), 4 ear shapes, 4 arm shapes, 1 bottom shape, 1 heart shape and 1 snout shape. Cut an additional 2 bottom shapes using scrap material, for the rice bag.

4 To make the rice bag, pin the pieces of scrap material together and sew, leaving a 2 cm (¾ in) hole for turning right side out (as marked). Turn right side out and fill bag with rice. Stitch hole closed and insert in the base of the knitted bunny.

5 Tack the remaining (patterned) bottom piece on to one side of the rice bag (right side out). Insert the

{bunny}

rice bag into the bunny's open base (right side of the patterned fabric facing out). Pin in place, with the knitted edge tucked over the top of the rice bag. Stitch securely.

6 For the legs, fold each piece in half (right sides facing) as indicated on the pattern and sew. Leave the base of each leg open for turning right side out and stuffing. Turn right side out.

7 Use a stuffing stick to stuff each leg, then hand stitch the openings closed. Tuck the legs under the edge of the bunny's front, about 2 cm (¾ in) apart (see photo). Pin and stitch in place.

8 Trace a mouth onto the white snout piece. Stitch the snout piece onto the bunny, placing it so that the top is in line with the top of the first CC stripe on the body (see photo). Pin on and stitch. Hand stitch the mouth with embroidery thread. Attach a button for the nose, then attach remaining buttons for the eyes (as shown in the photograph).

{bunny}

9 For each arm, pin 2 pieces together (right sides facing) and sew, leaving the ends open for turning right side out and stuffing. Turn right side out and use a stuffing stick to stuff each arm. Attach arms on each side of the body, positioning the top of the arms at the bottom edge of the second CC stripe (see photo).

10 For each ear, pin 2 pieces together (right sides facing) and sew, leaving the ends open for turning right side out and stuffing. Turn right side out. Using the dotted lines on the pattern as a guide, fold the front of each ear slightly and stitch it in place – this will give it the shape of a bunny ear. Attach ears on each side of the body, just above the eyes.

11 Attach the pompom tail on the back of the bunny, as shown in the photograph below.

12 Pin the heart shape onto the body (as shown in the photo) and stitch on.

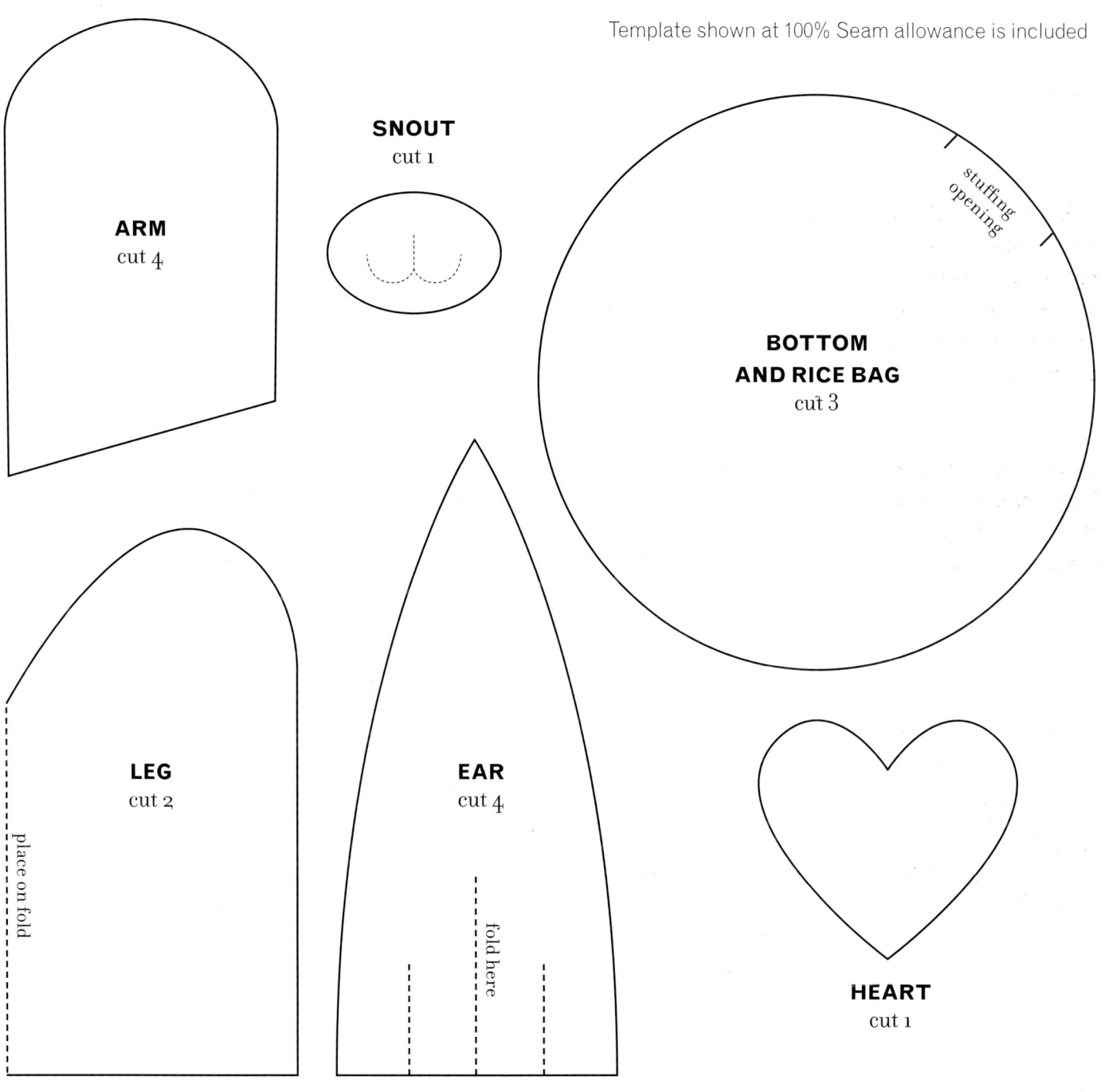

mabel monkey

{Hatch – prairiemouse.typepad.com/prairiemouse} LOUISE HATCHARD

Who doesn't love a cheeky monkey? With her sweet fabric and quizzical expression, Mabel is sure to inspire devotion from her owner!

FINISHED SIZE
29 cm × 15 cm (11½ in × 6 in) – excluding tail

TOOLS
- Tracing paper
- Scissors
- Pins
- Sewing needle
- Sewing machine
- Stuffing stick (or chopstick or pencil)
- Iron

MATERIALS
- Body fabric – a 35 cm × 35 cm (14 in × 14 in) piece of patterned cotton for head and body, and backs of ears.
- Extra fabric – a 35 cm × 35 cm (14 in × 14 in) piece of contrasting patterned cotton for arms, legs, fronts of ears and tail; a 12 cm × 12 cm (5 in × 5 in) piece of felt or fine woollen blanketing for face.
- Thread – sewing thread to match body fabric; embroidery thread in two colours of choice for face details.
- Decorations – one button.
- Stuffing – polyfill.

(CONTINUED)

{mabel monkey}

INSTRUCTIONS

1 Trace and cut out the enlarged pattern using the template provided. Pin it to the appropriate fabric and cut out the pieces. You will need to cut 2 head and body shapes, 4 arm shapes, 4 leg shapes, 2 tail shapes, 1 face shape and 4 ear shapes from your fabric. Remember that 2 of the ear shapes (for the backs of the ears) should be cut out of the body fabric, while the other 2 ear shapes (for the fronts of the ears) should be cut from the same fabric as the arms and legs.

2 For each arm, pin 2 pieces together (right sides facing) and sew, leaving the end open for turning right side out and stuffing. Repeat for legs, ears and tail. Turn all pieces right side out and iron. Stuff arms, legs and tail until stuffing is about 12 mm (½ in) from the opening (ears are not stuffed).

{mabel monkey}

3 Pin felt face piece onto head, then sew on by hand, using running stitch and three strands of embroidery thread. (I use an iron-on adhesive to apply the face before I sew it on – this also make embroidering the facial features easier.) Embroider a line across the nose from A to B. Embroider the mouth and nose in a different colour using back stitch and embroider the eyes with satin stitch (as marked on the pattern).

4 Place this head/body piece right side up on your work surface. Pin the limbs and ears in position (x to x, y to y and z to z), pointing in towards the body and remembering which way they will face when the body is turned right side out (see diagram on page 3). Place the second head/body piece right side down on top and pin the two pieces together. Sew, securing the limbs and ears in place as you go, and leaving an opening for turning right side out and stuffing (as marked on the pattern). Turn right side out.

5 Using a stuffing stick, push small amounts of stuffing into the head and body until the stuffing is firm and even, but not too tight.

6 Sew the stuffing opening closed using a small whip stitch.

7 Fold base of tail over about 5 mm (¼ in) and attach to the lower-middle of the back (as marked), using a small whip stitch. Sew a button of your choice through the base of the tail, or use a button covered with a small piece of the body fabric.

(CONTINUED)

Enlarge template to 125% Seam allowance is included

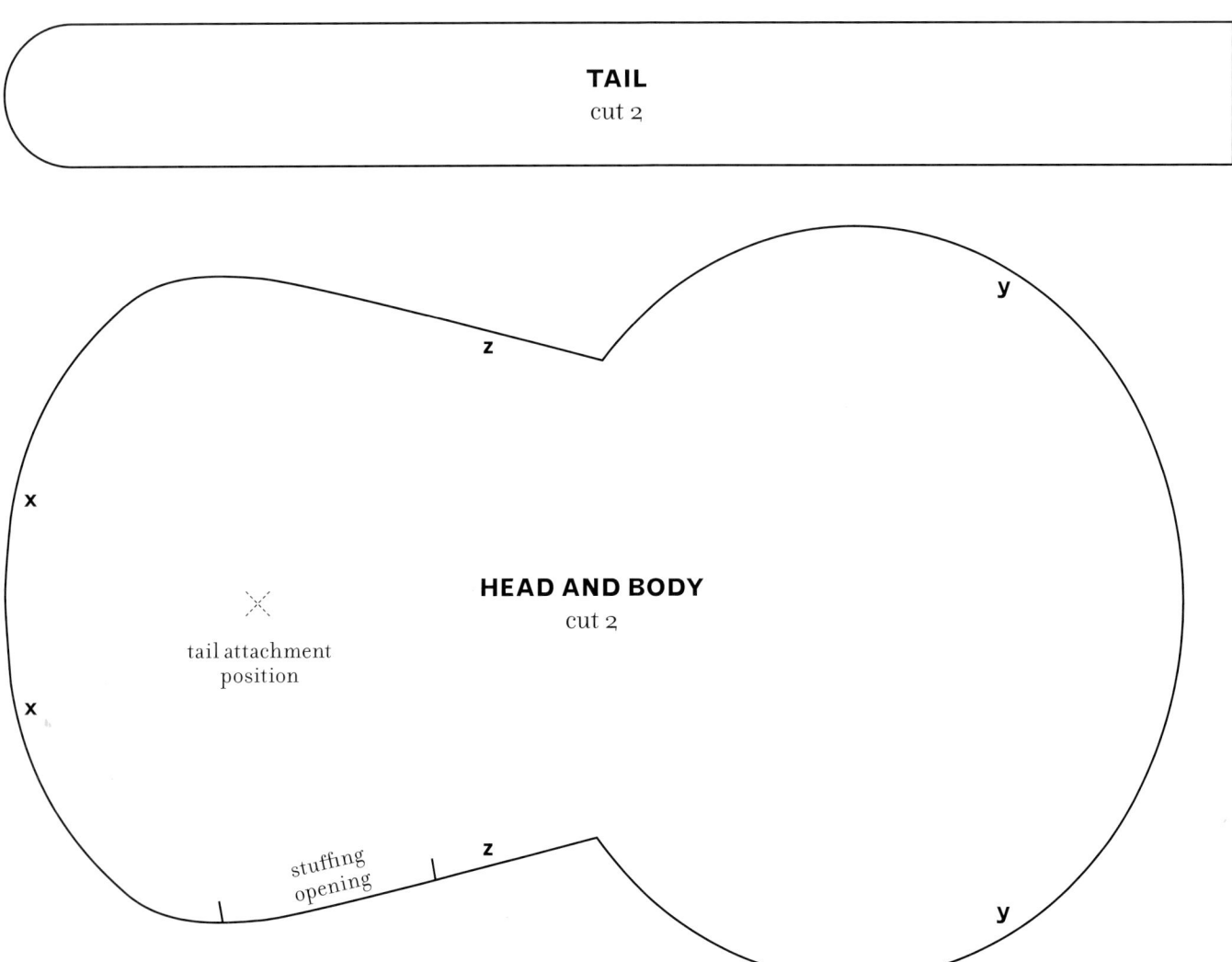

34 mabel monkey

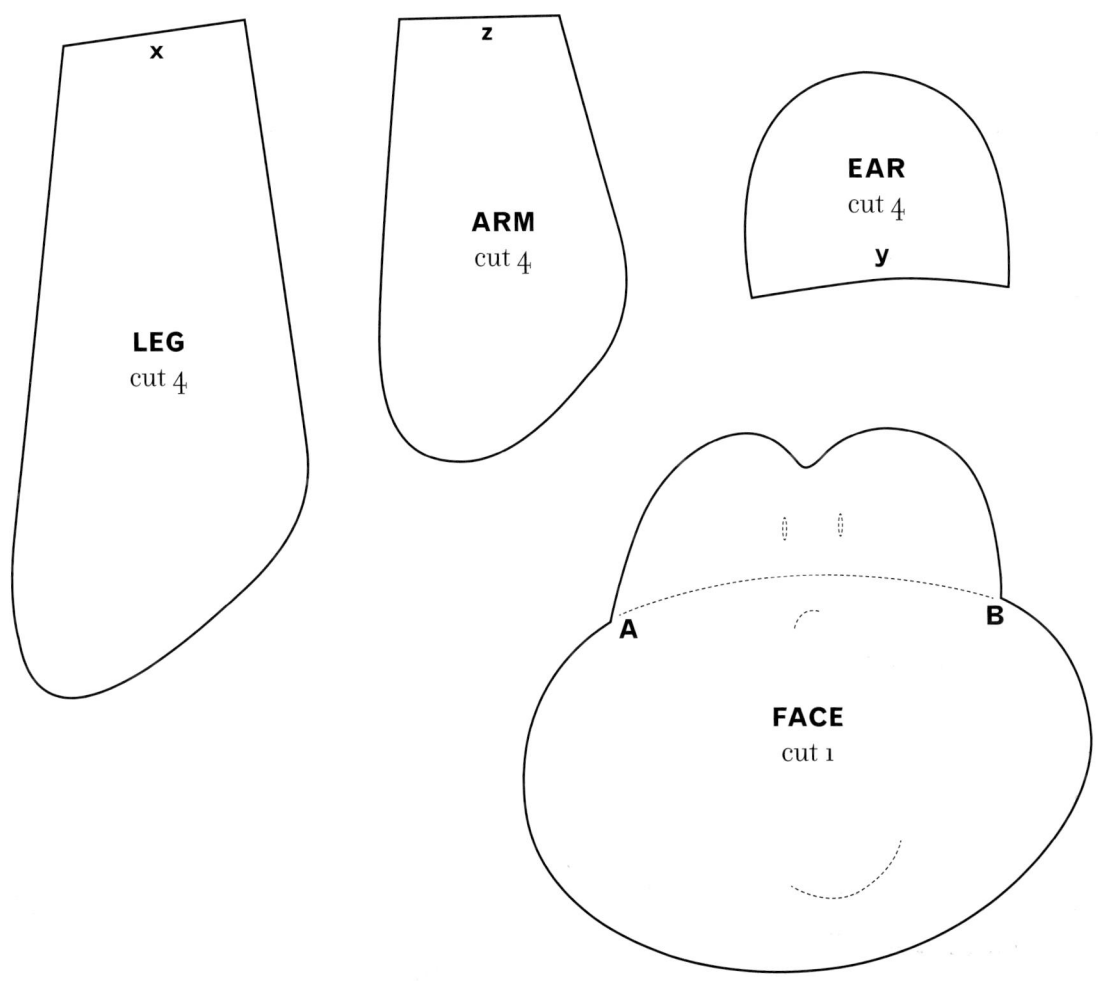

plurbit

{H. Love – mciverson.com} HEIDI IVERSON

Made with a variety of contrasting materials, I really enjoy the play on colour, pattern and texture in this toy. The possibilities are endless. If you decide to use alternative fabrics to those suggested here, just remember to avoid really stretchy fabrics or fabrics that fray easily.

FINISHED SIZE
24 cm × 17 cm (9½ in × 6½ in)

TOOLS
- Tracing paper
- Scissors
- Pinking shears
- Pins
- Sewing machine
- Tapestry needle

MATERIALS
- Body fabric – two 21 cm × 30 cm (8 in × 11 in) sheets of felt for the body and ears.
- Extra fabric – one 21 cm × 30 cm (8 in × 11 in) sheet of felt in a contrasting colour for the face mask; one 21 cm × 30 cm (8 in × 11 in) sheet of felt in another colour for the eyes; a scrap of felt for the mouth. (You can substitute calico cotton or vintage neck ties for the eyes and/or face).
- Yarn – angora, wool or cotton yarn in 2 colours that contrast with the body fabric.
- Thread – sewing thread in 3 or 4 different colours (one colour should match the body fabric, the others should be contrasting).
- Stuffing – polyfill.

{CONTINUED}

{plurbit}

INSTRUCTIONS

1 Trace and cut out the enlarged pattern using the template provided. Pin it to the chosen material and cut out the pieces. You will need to cut 2 body shapes, 1 face mask shape, 2 eye shapes (of slightly different sizes), 1 mouth shape and 2 ear shapes from your fabric. Use scissors to cut out the face, eyes and mouth, and use pinking shears to cut out the body and ears.

2 Pin face mask onto the head of the body (as marked on the pattern). Set sewing machine to zigzag satin stitch and use a contrasting thread colour to stitch the face mask onto the head.

3 Pin the eyes onto the face mask. Using a different coloured contrasting thread, satin-stitch the eyes onto the face mask.

4 Pin the mouth below the face mask, on the neck (as marked). Change thread colour again and satin-stitch mouth to body.

5 Using a tapestry needle and yarn, embroider a wide-spaced whip stitch, about 15 mm in length, all the way around the face mask.

6 Using tapestry needle and different coloured yarn, embroider a large X or line over each eye (see photo).

7 Pin body pieces together (wrong sides facing). Fold and pin-tuck the ears, then pin them into position between the two body pieces (x to x).

{plurbit}

8 Change the colour of the sewing thread to match the body fabric. Using a straight stitch, sew the body pieces together, securing the ears as you go. Leave a small opening between the ears for stuffing (as marked).

9 Using a stuffing stick, push small amounts of stuffing into the arms, legs and body first. Gradually fill the head until the stuffing is firm and even.

10 Hand sew the stuffing opening closed using a straight stitch or use the sewing machine.

Enlarge template to 130% Seam allowance is included

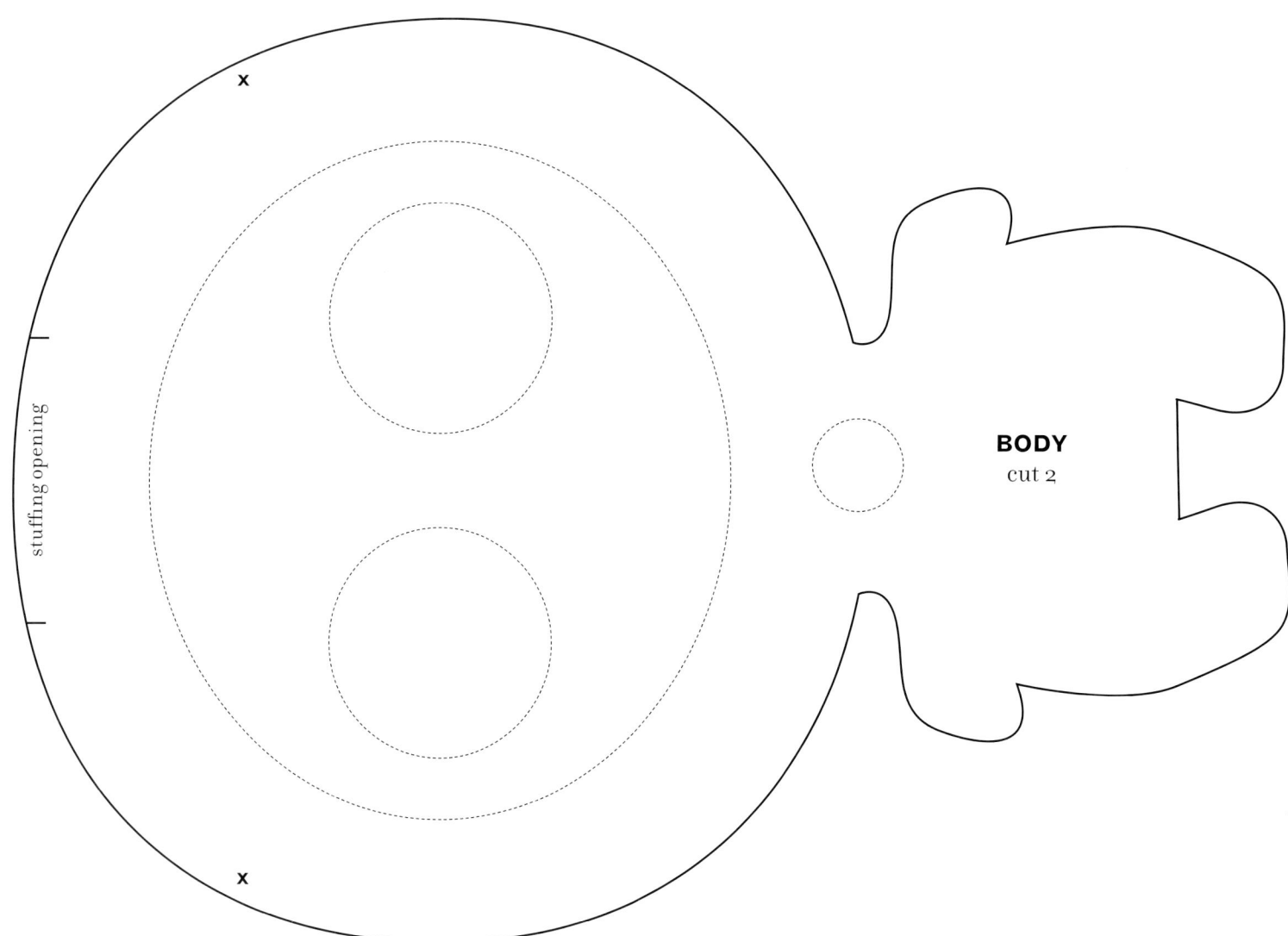

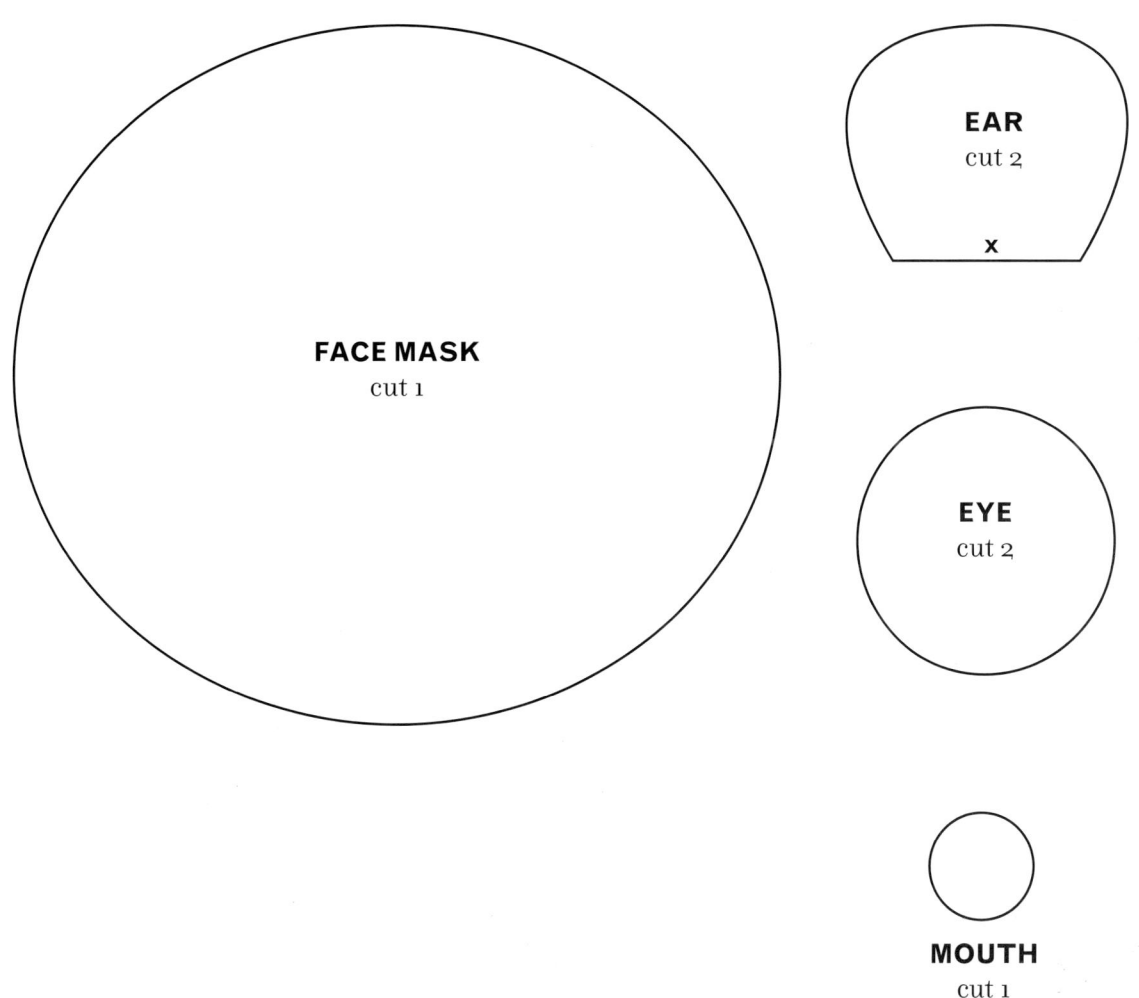

lizard

{while she naps – www.whileshenaps.typepad.com} ABIGAIL PATNER GLASSENBERG

This appealing little lizard is a jointed toy. Because small buttons are used to secure the limbs, it is not suitable for children under three years of age. Machine sewing is recommended for this toy – set the machine to a very small stitch length. If hand sewing, use a firm back stitch so that the seams will hold when the toy is stuffed.

FINISHED SIZE
4 cm × 19 cm (1½ in × 7½ in)

TOOLS
- Tracing paper
- Scissors
- Pins
- Small sewing needle
- Sewing machine
- Doll needle: 8–15 cm (3-6 in) doll needle
- Embroidery needle
- Stuffing stick (or chopstick or pencil)
- Iron
- Tweezers
- Hole puncher (optional, but makes neat circles for pupils)

MATERIALS
- Body fabric – a 25 cm × 25 cm (10 in × 10 in) piece of scrap fabric for the lizard's body and legs (or use contrasting material for the legs).
- Extra fabric – a scrap of light material for the gusset, plus small pieces of felt for the eyes (preferably wool felt), in two colours – light and dark.
- Thread – sewing thread to match colour of body fabric; extra-strong sewing thread for attaching the legs to the body; embroidery thread in contrasting colour.
- Decorations – 4 small shirt buttons to attach the limbs.
- Stuffing – preferably use wool rovings because they are a natural fibre and wear well, but you can substitute polyfill if you don't have wool.

(CONTINUED)

{lizard}

INSTRUCTIONS

1 Trace and cut out the pattern using the template provided. Pin it to the chosen fabric and cut out the pieces. You will need to cut 8 leg shapes, 1 gusset shape, and 2 body shapes. Do not cut out the eyes yet.

2 Place the gusset piece and one body piece together (right sides facing), and align at points A and B (marked on the pattern). Sew from A to B to attach the gusset to the body piece. Repeat to attach remaining body piece to the other side of the gusset. Starting at B, sew down the lizard's tail to join the body together, leaving an opening (as marked) for turning right side out and stuffing. Trim all curves close to the stitch line to allow for a smoother finish after turning right side out. Check seams for areas that may need reinforcing. Carefully turn right side out, pulling the head out first and then tail.

3 Using a stuffing stick, push small amounts of stuffing into the tight corners first – tail and head. Stuff the body firmly. Hand sew neat ladder stitch to close the stuffing opening.

4 For each leg, pin 2 pieces together (right sides facing) and sew, leaving an opening as marked on the pattern for turning right side out and stuffing. Trim all curves close to the stitch line (take special care when clipping between the toes). Using tweezers, carefully turn the feet right side out. This may take some patience because the feet are small. Using a stuffing stick, push small amounts of stuffing into the toes and feet, stuffing firmly. Then sew across each foot at the dotted line marked on the pattern. This will create a flat foot. Firmly stuff the remainder of the legs. Hand sew a neat ladder stitch to close the stuffing opening.

To make the feet stay pointing forward, bend the foot up until it touches the leg. Use small stitches to secure the foot so it will stay facing forward and won't flop down when the toy is picked up.

5 To attach the legs to the body, thread the doll needle with extra-strong thread. Pass the needle through the body where one of the back legs will go (at x), then through the side seam of one leg, and finally through a hole in a shirt button. Pass the needle back through a second hole in the button, through the side seam of the leg and back through the body, coming out on the

{lizard}

opposite side of the body. Repeat the process going through the other back leg and its button, back through the button and leg and through the lizard. Go back and forth a few times until all button holes are used and lizard's back legs are attached very firmly. Wrap thread around a button a few times and tie off. Repeat with front legs (at y). Lizard should now be able to stand on its own legs.

6 For the eyes, cut three 15-mm circles from the light-coloured felt. Cut one of these circles in half to form the two eyelids. Cut or use a hole puncher to punch out two smaller circles from dark-coloured felt for the pupils. Place one dark circle in the centre of one light circle. Fit the eyelid piece on top of the pupil. Sew the pupil to the eye and sew the eyelid to the pupil. Sew eyes onto lizard (as shown in the photographs) using tiny stitches.

7 Embroider eyebrows with contrasting embroidery thread, using two straight stitches to make an inverted-V-shaped eyebrow.

Template shown at 100% Seam allowance is included

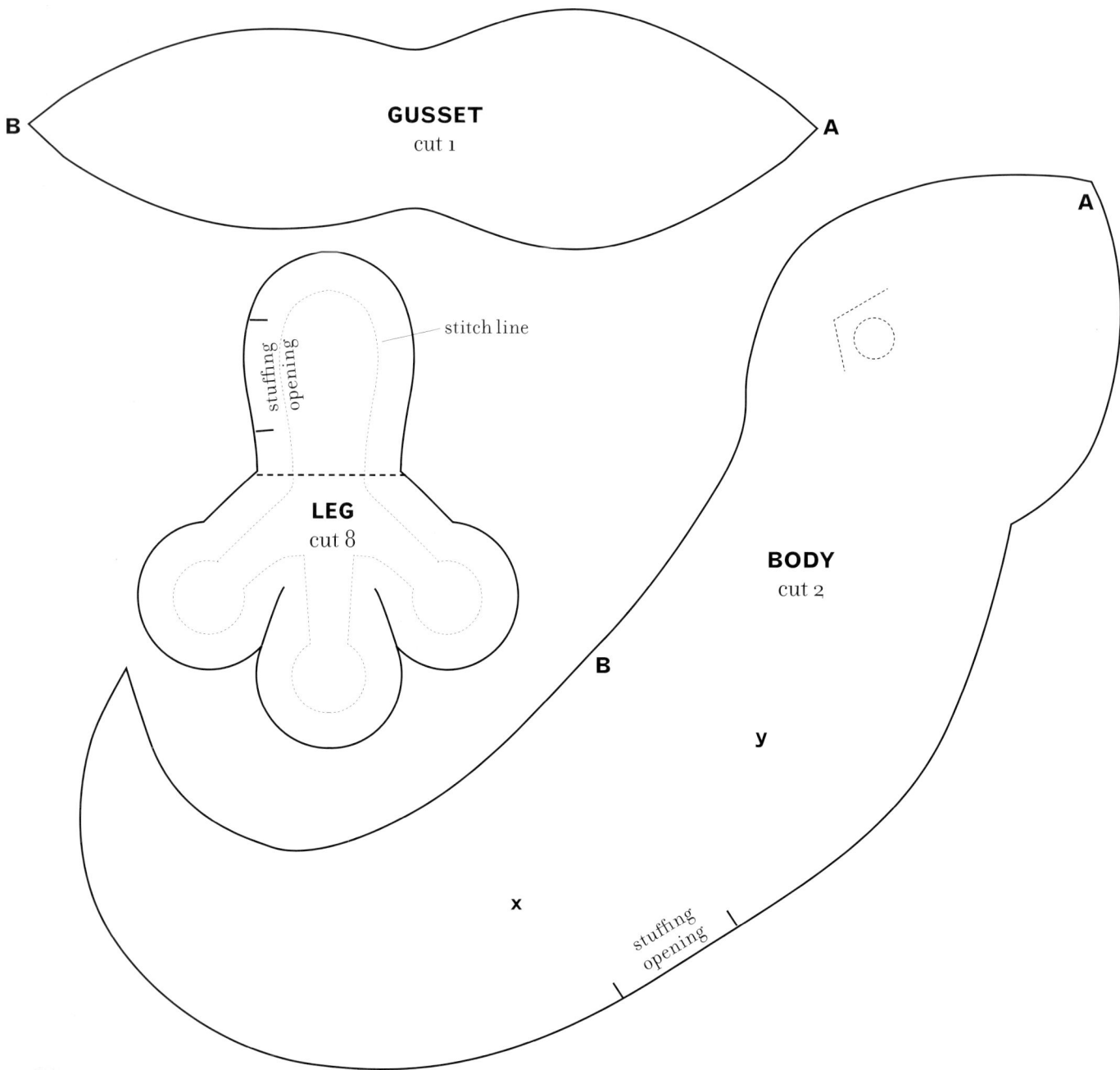

henny house

{Hatch – www.prairiemouse.typepad.com/prairie mouse} LOUISE HATCHARD

Be creative with the fabrics you use for this toy – enjoy putting together different colours, patterns and textures. Add buttons and beads (for children over three) and embroidery. Have fun, and remember to take a photo of your creation for your records if you are giving it away as a gift.

FINISHED SIZE
23 cm × 16 cm (9 in × 6 in)

TOOLS
- Tracing paper
- Scissors
- Pins
- Sewing needle
- Sewing machine
- Stuffing stick (or chopstick or pencil)
- Iron

MATERIALS
- Body fabric – a 15 cm × 15 cm (6 in × 6 in) piece of linen for front of house; a 16 cm × 25 cm (6½ in × 10 in) piece of patterned cotton for back of house and legs; a 12 cm × 30 cm (5 in × 12 in) piece of patterned cotton for roof.
- Extra fabric – a 13 cm × 10 cm (5 in × 4 in) piece of patterned cotton for arms (can be the same as back/legs or different); scraps of felt or fine woollen blanketing for window and shutters; a small piece of patterned cotton for heart.
- Thread – sewing thread in 2 colours (1 to match fabric, and 1 in a contrasting colour); embroidery thread for the face details.
- Decorations – ric rac or braid.
- Stuffing – polyfill.

(CONTINUED)

{henny house}

INSTRUCTIONS

1 Trace and cut out the pattern using the template provided. Pin it to the appropriate fabric and cut out the pieces. You will need to cut 2 body shapes, 4 leg shapes, 2 roof shapes, 4 arm shapes, 1 window shape, 2 shutter shapes and 1 heart shape from your fabric.

2 For each leg, pin 2 pieces together (right sides facing) and sew, leaving the end open for turning right side out and stuffing. Repeat for arms. Turn arms and legs right side out and iron. Using a stuffing stick, push small amounts of stuffing into arms and legs until stuffing is about 12 mm (½ in) from the top.

3 Pin each roof piece to a body piece (right sides facing) and sew. Iron seams flat.

4 On the right side of one of the body pieces, embroider the mouth using stem stitch and three strands of embroidery thread. Then use satin stitch to embroider the eyes (as shown on pattern).

5 Machine stitch the ric rac or braid under the roof line (as marked). Hand stitch on the heart piece using a running stitch and embroidery thread. Sew the shutters on with small stitches in a contrasting embroidery thread colour, then use back stitch to attach the window. (I like to use an iron-on adhesive to apply the window, shutters and heart, before I sew them.)

6 Place this roof/body piece right side up on your work surface. Pin the arms and legs into position (x to x and y to y), pointing in towards the body and remembering which way they will face when the body is turned right side out (see diagram on page 3). Place the second roof/body piece right side down on top and pin the two pieces together. Sew, securing the limbs as you go, and leaving an opening for turning right side out and stuffing (as marked). Turn right side out and iron.

7 Using a stuffing stick, push small amounts of stuffing into the house until firm. Hand sew the stuffing opening closed using a very small whip stitch.

{CONTINUED}

Template shown at 100% Seam allowance is included

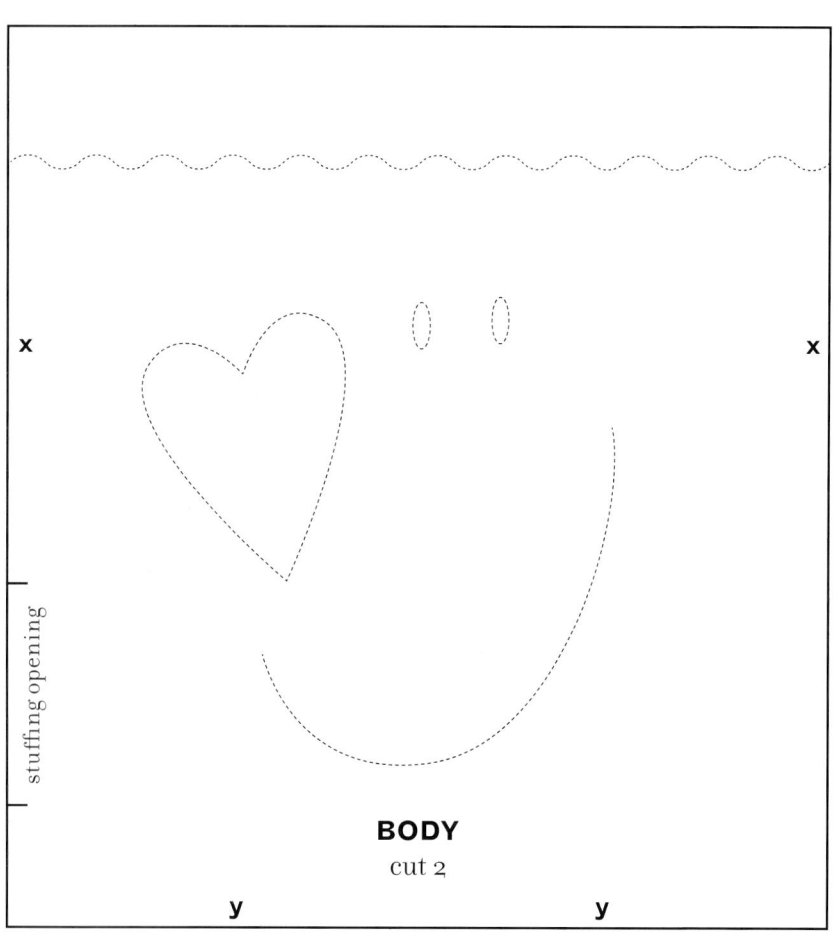

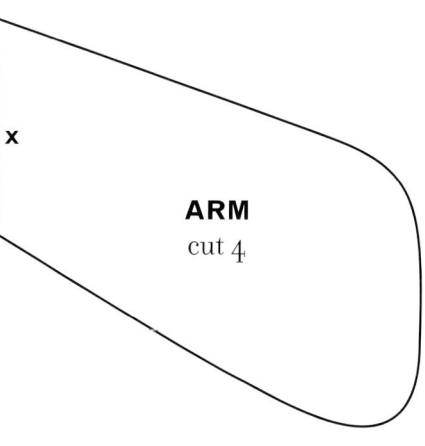

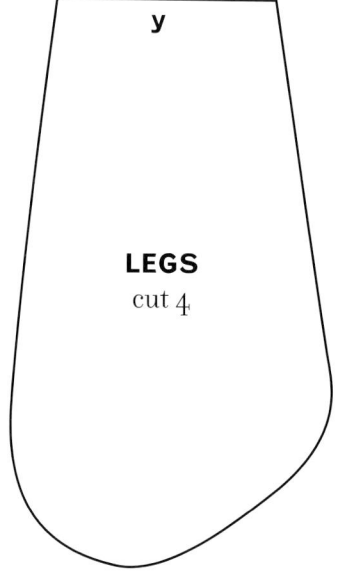

50 henny house

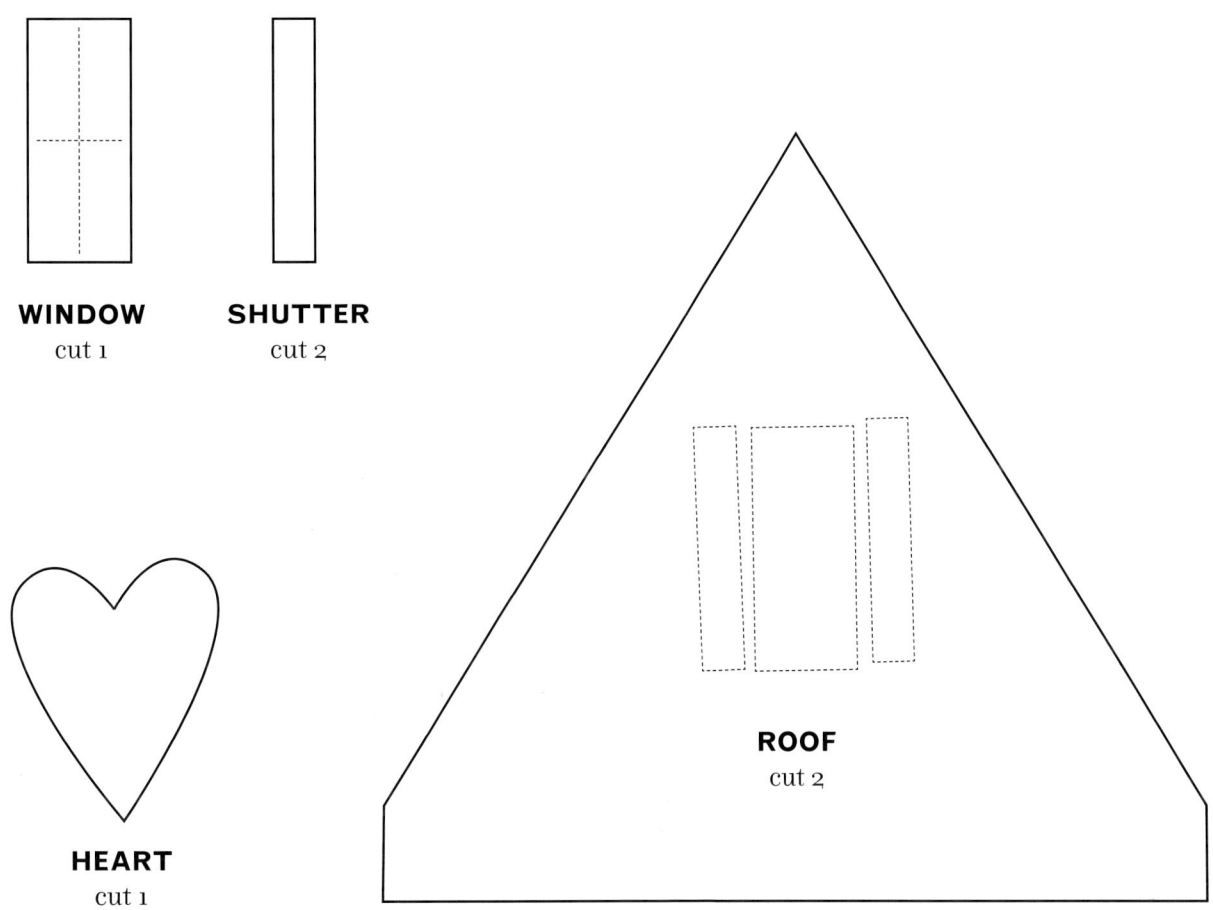

henny house

guardian angel

{herzensart — www.herzensart.com} SANDRA MONAT

The themes in my work are influenced by my love of the spiritual and symbolic, mythology and animals. Guardian angels are spiritual beings that are 'assigned' to assist people here on earth in various ways. They come to our aid in times of great need. This friendly angel toy is made to remind you of your very own guardian angel. It shall bring joy and peace to your home.

FINISHED SIZE
26 cm × 33 cm (10 in × 13 in)

TOOLS
- Tracing paper
- Scissors
- Pins
- Sewing needle
- Sewing machine
- Stuffing stick (or chopstick or pencil)

MATERIALS
- Body fabric – a 30 cm × 60 cm (12 in × 24 in) piece of heavy-duty modern or vintage patterned fabric (e.g. corduroy).
- Extra fabric – a small piece of white felt (or other non-fraying fabric) for the face and hands; a small piece of patterned linen fabric for the nose; scrap material for the cheeks in plain pink, orange or red; a piece of cotton, felt or bouclé for the legs; a 40 cm × 45 cm (16 in × 18 in) piece of strong cotton fabric for the wings in a plain colour, such as yellow or orange.
- Thread – sewing thread in 1 or more colours; embroidery thread for embroidering the face (dark-brown, grey or black for the eyes; red, pink or orange for the mouth); extra-strong thread for attaching the wings.
- Stuffing – polyfill.

{CONTINUED}

{guardian angel}

INSTRUCTIONS

1 Trace and cut out the enlarged pattern using the template provided. Pin it to the appropriate fabric and cut out the pieces. You will need to cut 2 body shapes, 4 leg shapes, 2 hand shapes, 2 wing shapes, 1 face shape, 2 cheek shapes and 1 nose shape from your fabric.

2 Pin the face piece onto the right side of one of the body pieces, about 1.5 cm in from the top edge (as marked on the pattern). Sew the face to the body using a small zigzag stitch.

3 Pin the hand pieces to the right side of the body fabric (right side facing out), as shown on the pattern. Set the sewing machine to a zigzag stitch and sew around each hand from A to B.

4 Choose a decorative stitch and sew a line horizontally from C to B across the top of each hand. Then sew from B to D.

5 Attach the nose and cheek pieces to the face, either using a small zigzag stitch on the sewing machine, or by hand.

6 Using a dark-coloured thread, embroider the eyes as shown on the pattern. Use red, pink or orange thread to embroider a mouth.

7 For each leg, pin 2 pieces together (right sides facing) and sew. Leave the top of each leg open for turning right side out and stuffing. With scissors, trim fabric where the foot curves. Be careful not to clip the seam. Turn right side out.

8 Using a stuffing stick, push small amounts of stuffing into each leg. Hand stitch the stuffing opening closed.

9 Pin the wing pieces together (right sides facing) and sew, leave an opening for turning right side out and stuffing (as shown on the pattern). With scissors, clip fabric around the curved edges. Be careful not to clip the seam. Turn right side out.

{guardian angel}

10 Using a stuffing stick, stuff the wings. Hand stitch the opening closed.

11 Place the front side of the angel's body right side up on your work surface. Pin the legs into position (x to x), pointing in towards the body and remembering which way they will face when the body is turned right side out (see diagram on page 3). Place the second body piece right side down on top and pin the two pieces together. Sew around the body, remembering to leave an opening between the legs for turning right side out and stuffing (as marked). After sewing, use scissors to clip fabric around the curved edges. Turn right side out.

12 Using a stuffing stick, stuff the body firmly. Hand stitch the stuffing opening closed.

13 Use a strong thread and large stitches to hand-sew the wings onto the back of the angel's body, as shown in the photograph. Make sure they are firmly attached.

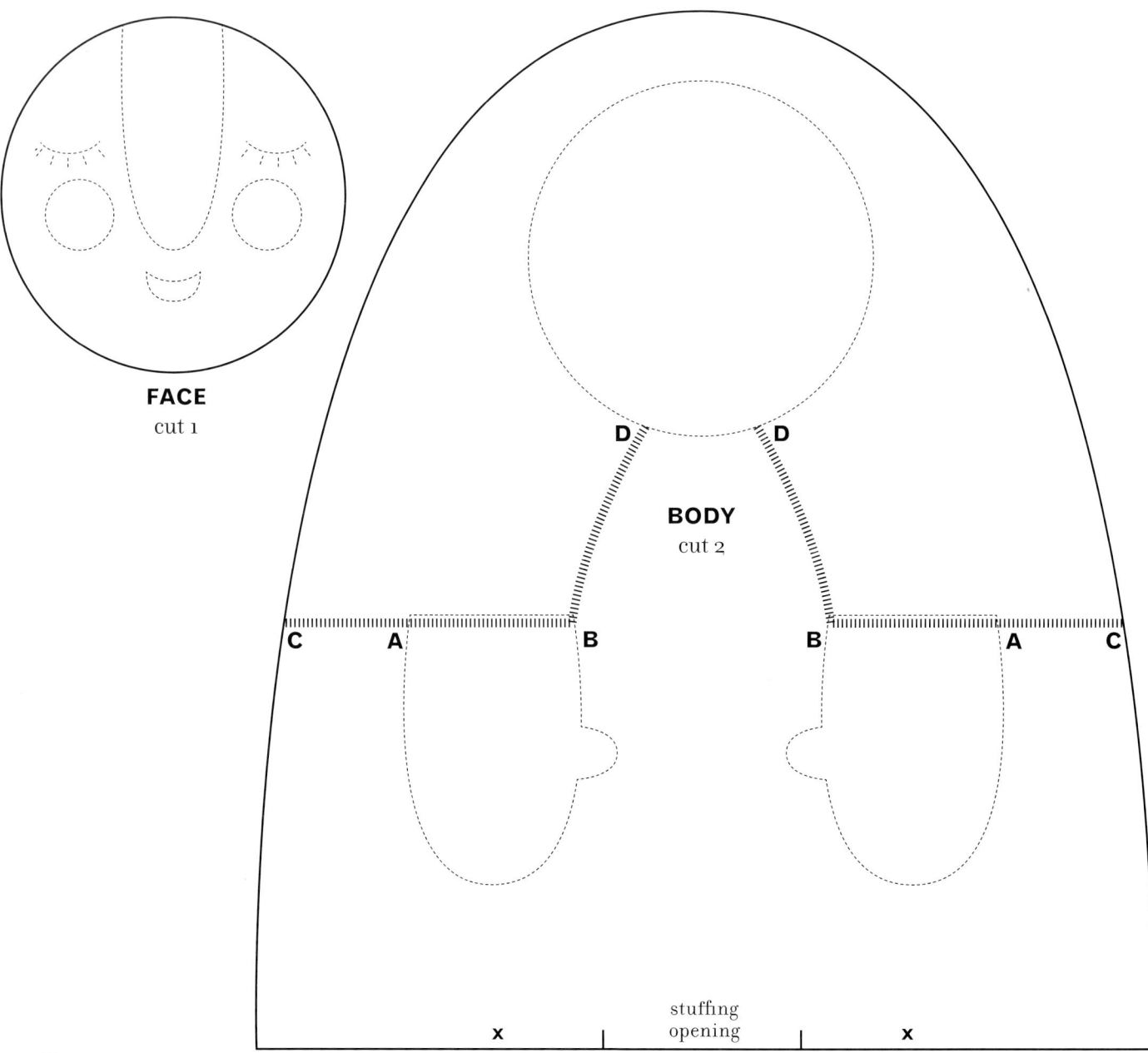

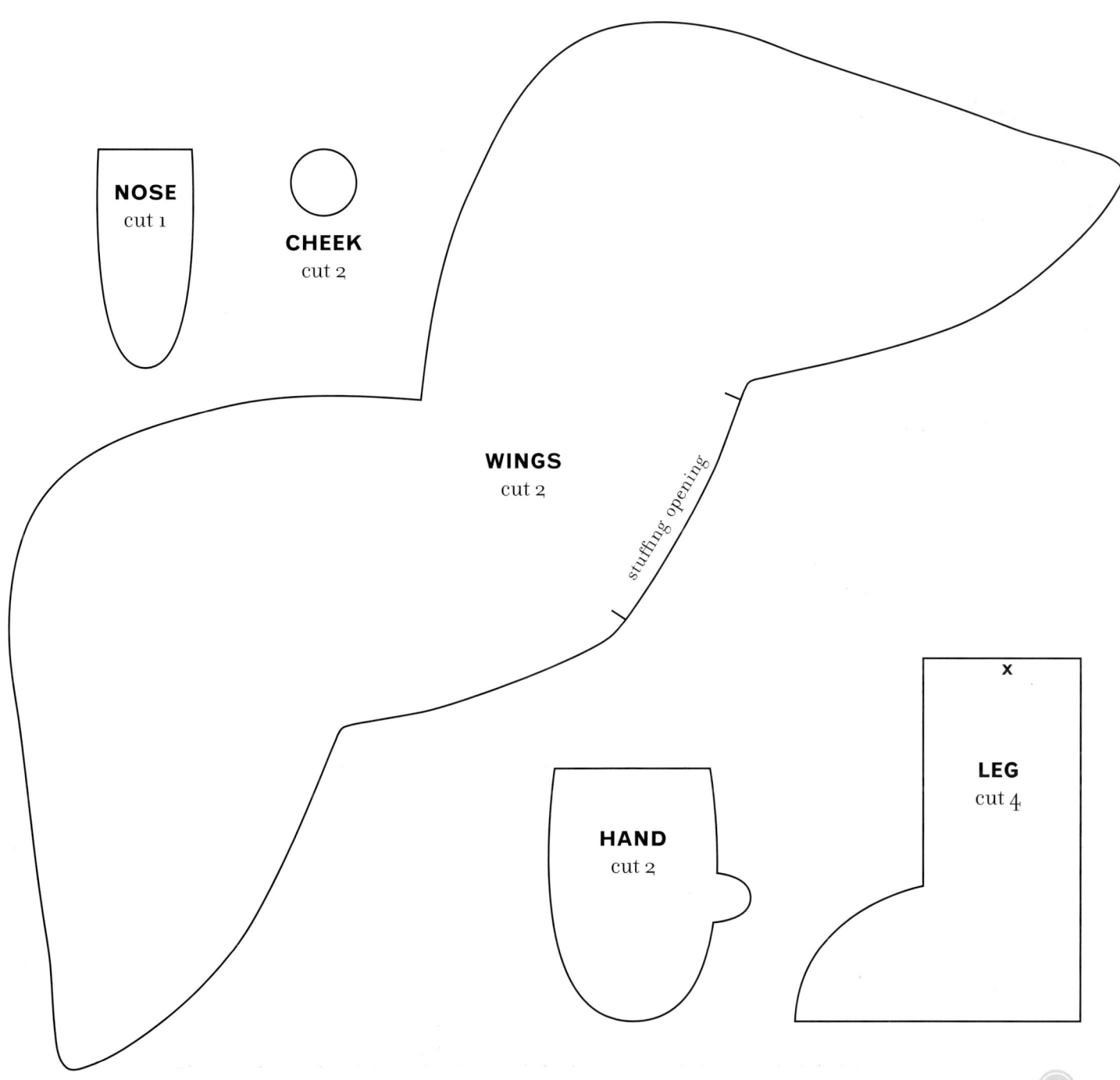

guardian angel 57

arno cat

{Soozs – www.soozs.blogspot.com} SUZIE FRY

I developed the pattern for this super-easy soft toy when I was living in Thailand. At that time I didn't have a sewing machine or many tools, so I was thinking simple and quick. The body is made up of two identical pieces so there's no complicated fitting lines and no limbs or attachments, so it is suitable for hand sewing by an absolute beginner. Of course you can use a machine as well if you have one handy. Although I have given instructions for how to do the face detailing, there's no end to the number of ways Arno can be embellished. This is not a precision toy, so don't worry about getting everything exactly right – each Arno I make has its own look and personality.

FINISHED SIZE
14 cm × 11 cm (5½ in × 4 in)

TOOLS
- Tracing paper
- Scissors
- Pins
- Sewing needle and/or machine
- Stuffing stick (or chopstick or pencil)

MATERIALS
- Body fabric – two 15 cm × 20 cm (6 in × 8 in) pieces of cotton. I prefer to use loosely woven heavyweight cotton because I think it has more 'give' than more tightly woven lightweight cotton. However, the weave needs to be tight enough to make sure the stuffing doesn't show or come loose. You can also use felt or a stretch fabric, though you would need to adjust the seam allowance to 2–3 mm (1/12 in).
- Extra fabric – small pieces of contrast fabric for the face (lightweight cotton or felt), and felt for the eyes.
- Thread – coloured sewing thread to match the body and face fabric, plus embroidery thread for face detailing.
- Stuffing – preferably use wool rovings because they are a natural fibre and wear well, but you can substitute polyfill if you don't have wool.

{CONTINUED}

{arno cat}

INSTRUCTIONS

1 Trace and cut out the pattern using the template provided. Pin it to the fabric and cut out the pieces. You will need to cut 2 body shapes, 1 face shape (remember to eliminate the 6 mm seam allowance if you are using felt), and 2 eye shapes.

2 If you are using cotton for the face plate you will need to turn a small seam to stop it fraying: sew a fine running stitch around the edge of the fabric and then gently pull the thread to gather the material and turn the edge of the fabric over. You might find it helpful to cut a piece of paper to the shape of the finished face and use this as a guide.

3 Attach the face plate to one of the body pieces using a simple running stitch. In the striped version shown here, I have used a thread of matching colour, but you could use a contrasting colour to show off the stitches if you prefer.

4 Attach the felt eyes with thread of a contrasting colour and embroider a mouth and nose with embroidery thread. I like to add a cross-stitch in a contrasting colour for a belly button. You might also like to add some embroidered detail to the ears and paws, or even attach a tail.

5 Pin the two body pieces together (right sides facing) and sew, remembering to leave a portion of the seam open for turning right side out and stuffing (as marked on the pattern). After sewing, trim all curves close to the stitch line to allow for a smoother finish after turning right side out. Turn right side out. (If you're using a stiff felt, pin and sew together with wrong sides facing, leaving an opening for stuffing - this means you won't have to turn it right side out.)

6 Using a stuffing stick, push small amounts of stuffing into the tight corners first – ears, arms and legs. Gradually fill the rest of the body until the stuffing is firm and even, but not too tight.

7 Sew the stuffing opening closed using a whip stitch.

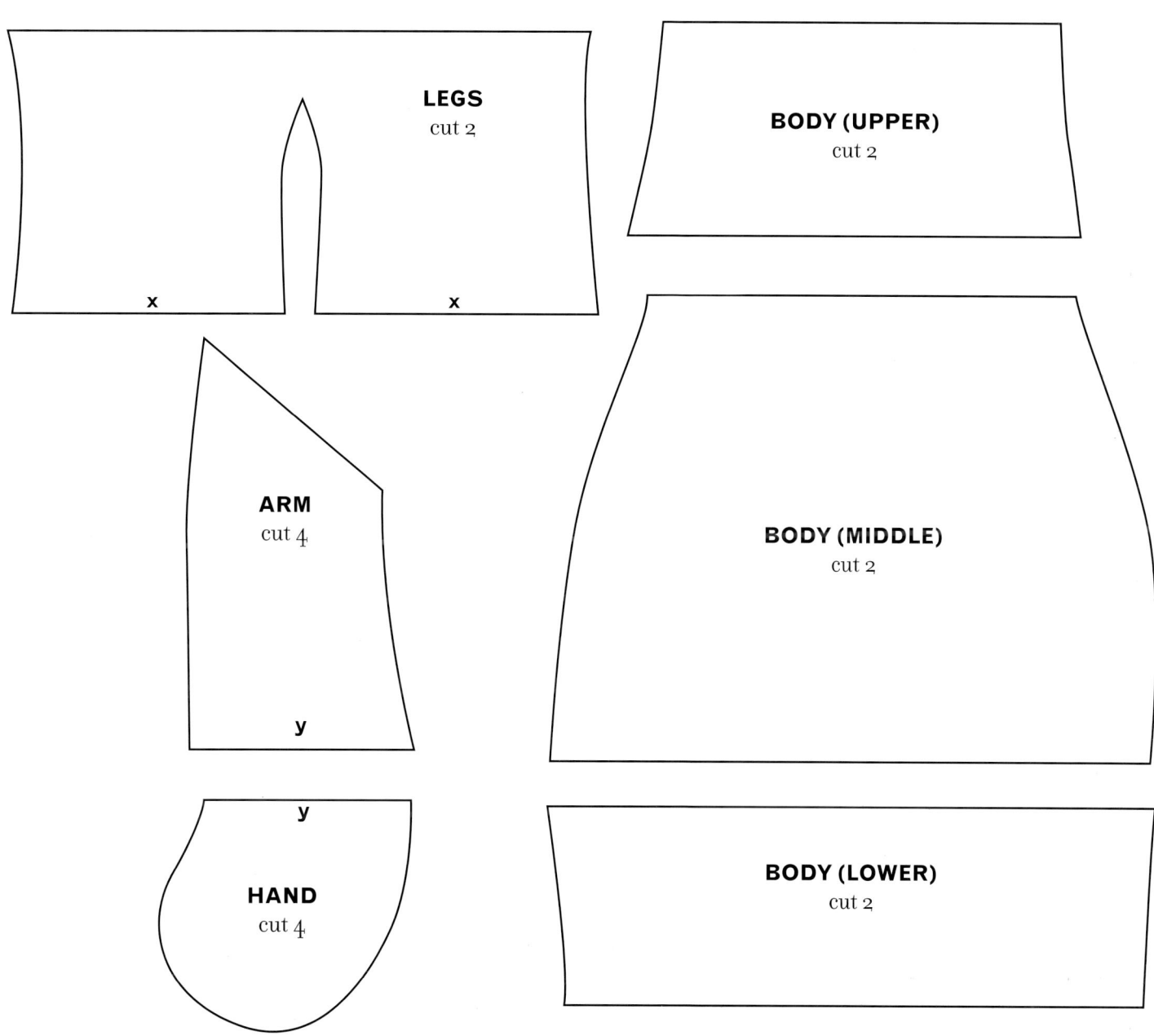

mamma bear

{Nest Studio – neststudio.typepad.com} CARLY SCHWERDT

A new take on an old favourite, Mamma Bear is funky and modern, but is just as nice to cuddle as any old-fashioned teddy bear.

FINISHED SIZE
24 cm × 12 cm (9½ in × 5 in) – legs and arms excluded

TOOLS
- Tracing paper
- Scissors
- Pins
- Sewing needle
- Sewing machine
- Stuffing stick (or chopstick or pencil)

MATERIALS
- Body fabric – 2 fat quarters of quality cotton fabric for the body.
- Extra fabric – a fat quarter of striped fabric for the legs; a fat quarter of wool blanketing for the head, arms and feet; scraps of cotton fabric for the hands; scraps of felt in beige, cream or brown for the eyes and nose.
- Thread – black sewing thread.
- Stuffing – polyfill or wool rovings.

(CONTINUED)

{mamma bear}

INSTRUCTIONS

1 Trace and cut out the enlarged pattern using the template provided. Pin it to the appropriate fabric and cut out the pieces. (I like to cut freehand without a pattern, as it makes for individual quirky toys – you can try this, using the pattern as a rough guide). You will need to cut 2 body shapes, 2 head shapes, 4 leg shapes, 4 arm shapes, 2 eye shapes, 4 foot shapes, 4 hand shapes and 1 nose shape from your fabric.

2 Pin each foot piece to a leg piece, x to x, (right sides facing) and sew together with the sewing machine. For each leg, sew 2 leg/foot pieces together (right sides facing), leaving a small opening as indicated on the pattern for turning right side out and stuffing. Repeat this process for arms and hands (sewing the hands to the arms, y to y). Turn right side out.

3 For the face, use sewing thread to neatly sew the felt eyes onto one of the woollen head pieces (as marked). Embroider nose and pupils (as shown on the pattern).

4 Pin each head piece to a body piece (right sides facing) and sew.

5 Place the front head/body piece right side up on your work surface. Pin the arms and legs into position (z to z and o to o), pointing in towards the body and remembering which way they will face when the body is turned right side out (see diagram on page 3). Make sure the stuffing openings in the limbs end up on the underside of the arms and the insides of the legs (so they show the least). Place the second head/body piece right side down on top and pin the two pieces together. Sew all around the body and head, securing the arms and legs as you go, and leaving a 4 cm (1½ in) opening for turning right side out and stuffing (as marked). (I always double stitch over the arms and legs, to make them extra strong.)

6 Trim all edges, but leave at least a 10 mm (⅖ in) border. With scissors, clip fabric around the curved edges. Be careful not to clip the seam. Turn right side out (take your time, as this can be a bit tricky).

{mamma bear}

7 Using a stuffing stick, push small amounts of stuffing into the ears first. Gradually fill the rest of the body until the stuffing is firm and even, but not too tight.

8 Sew the stuffing opening closed using a whip stitch.

Apron

MATERIALS
- Fabric – scraps of patterned fabric in 2 or more complementary colours.
- Thread – Sewing thread to match fabric.

INSTRUCTIONS
1 Trace and cut out the pattern using the template provided. Pin it to the fabric and cut out the pieces. You will need to cut 2 apron shapes. Also cut out a thin strip of fabric measuring 2 cm × 55 cm (¾ in × 22 in) for the apron tie.

2 Pin apron pieces together (right sides facing) and sew, leaving the top edge open. Turn right side out.

3 Fold both long edges of the tie piece into the centre (wrong sides together), and iron flat. Then fold in half lengthways and iron again. Pin top edge of apron piece between the fold, in the centre of the tie. Sew all along the length of the tie, securing the apron as you go.

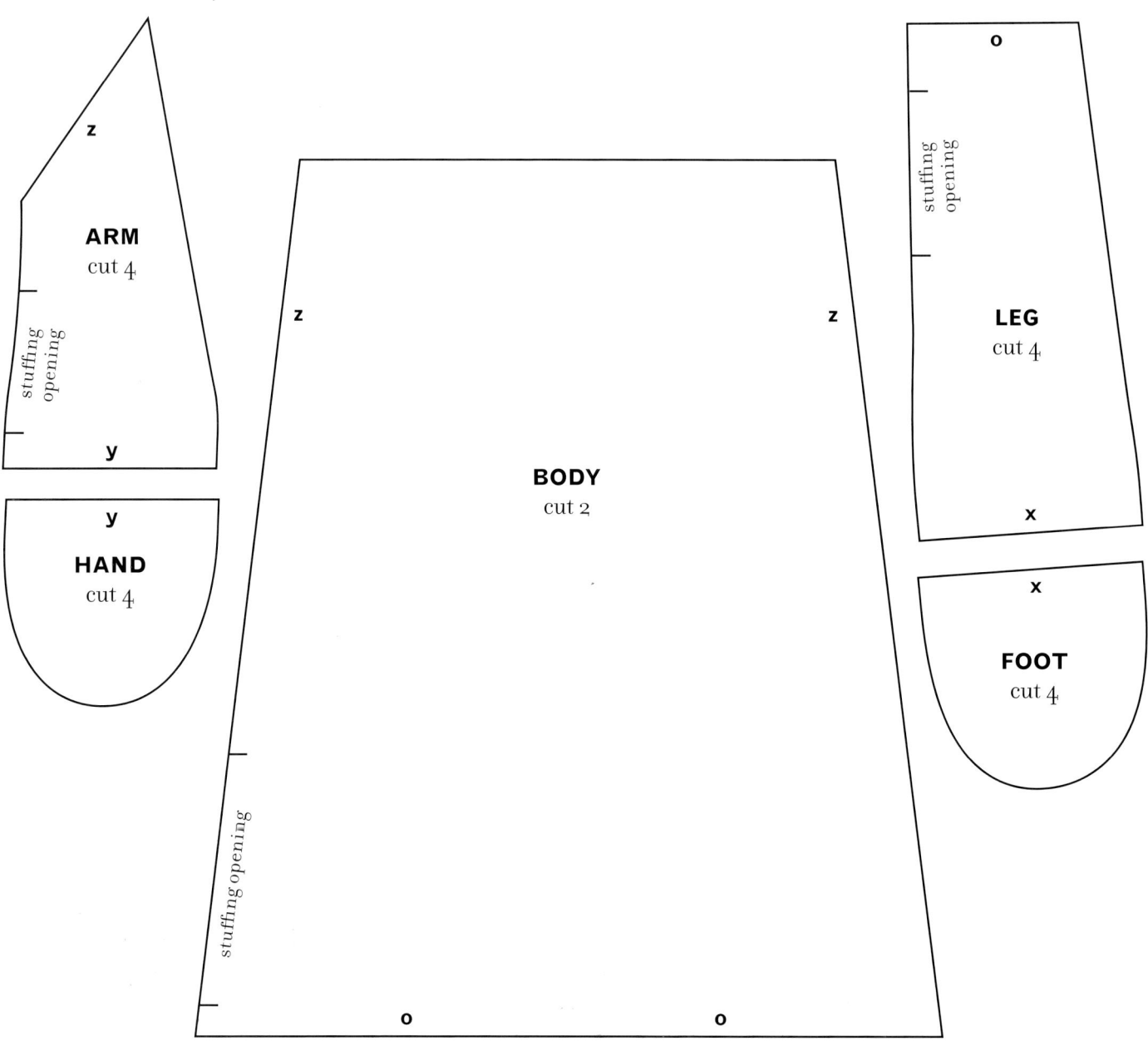

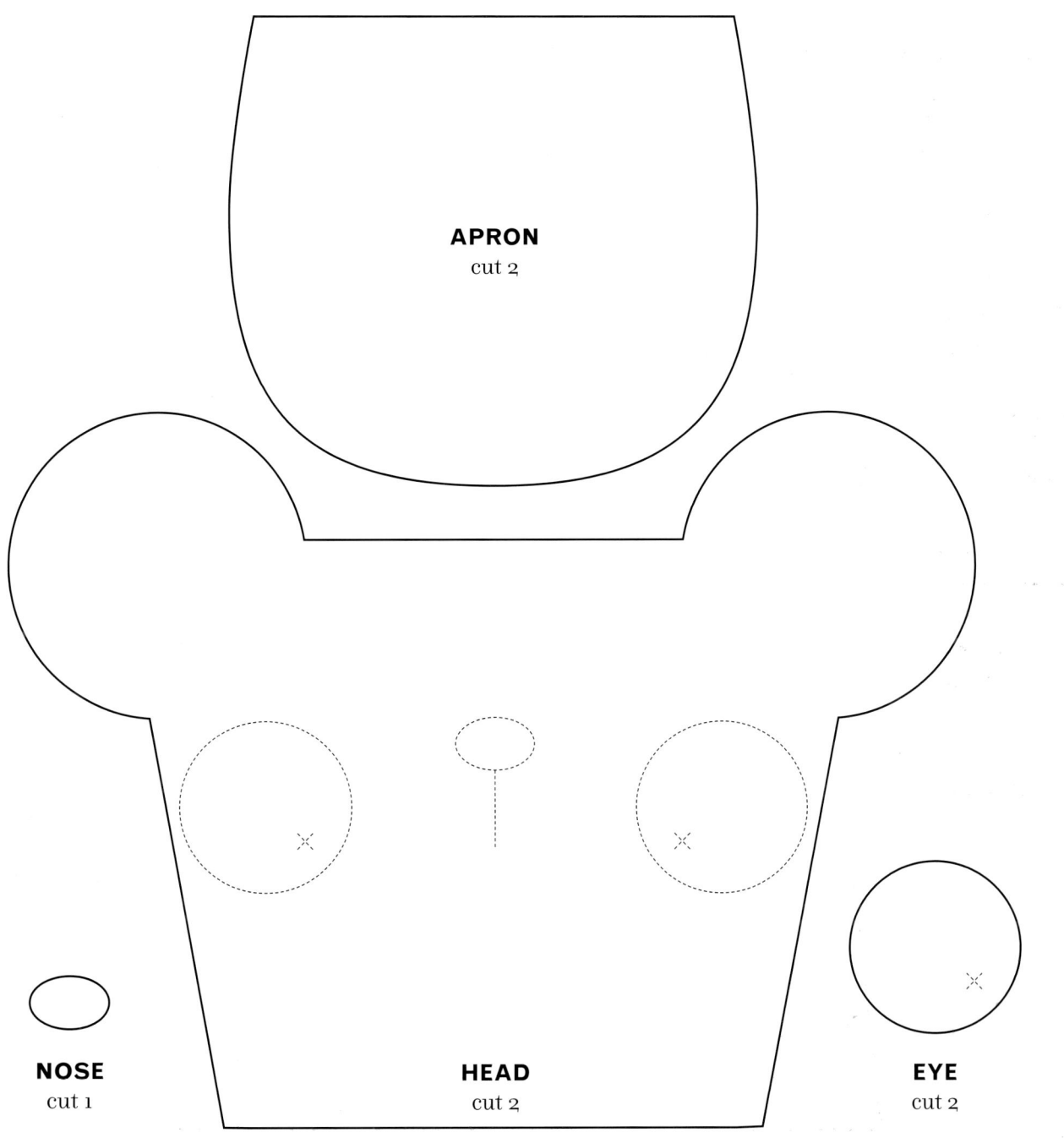

kangaroo

{My Little Mochi – mylittlemochi.typepad.com} MYRA MASUDA

Avoid bulkier fabrics when sewing this toy, as they will be hard to turn – especially for the little joey finger puppet. For best results, baste pieces before sewing.

FINISHED SIZE
20 cm × 14 cm (8 in × 5½ in) – ears excluded

TOOLS
- Iron
- Tracing paper
- Scissors
- Pins
- Sewing needle
- Sewing machine
- Stuffing stick (or chopstick or pencil)
- Tweezers

MATERIALS
- Body fabric – a 22 cm × 50 cm (7 in × 20 in) piece of plain fabric for the main body; an 18 cm × 30 cm (7 in × 12 in) piece of new or vintage patterned fabric for the inner body.
- Extra fabric – scraps of white felt for the eyes and black felt for the pupils; interfacing for the ears.
- Thread – coloured sewing thread to match the body fabric; black, pink and white embroidery thread for the face details.
- Stuffing – polyfill.

{CONTINUED}

{kangaroo}

INSTRUCTIONS

1 Trace and cut out the pattern using the template provided. Pin it to the fabric and cut out the pieces. You will need to cut 2 main body shapes, 1 inner body shape, 6 ear shapes (2 in each fabric, plus 2 in interfacing), 1 chin shape, 1 pouch shape (cut on the fold), 2 eye shapes and 2 pupil shapes from your fabric.

2 Pin main body pieces together (right sides facing) and sew around the top of the body from A to B, leaving an opening for turning inside out and stuffing, as marked on the pattern.

3 Pin the chin piece to the inner body piece (x to x), right sides facing, and sew together. Iron seam flat.

4 For the pouch, fold in half (right sides facing) and sew across the bottom from C to D (as indicated by the stitch line marked). Trim, then turn right side out and iron.

5 Line up the folded edge of the pouch with the top pouch placement line on the right side of the inner body piece, as indicated on the pattern. Line the side edges up with the sides of the inner body piece. Pin in place. This should create a slight gape at the top of the pouch. Sew down the sides of the pouch, 3 mm (⅛ in) in from the edge of the fabric on each side. Line up the bottom (sewn) edge of the pouch with the bottom pouch placement line, and hand sew along the bottom using a ladder stitch.

6 Pin the inner body/chin piece to the main body piece (right sides facing), A to A and B to B. Sew together.

7 Trim and clip fabric around the curved edges. Be careful not to clip the seam. Turn right side out.

8 Using a stuffing stick, push small amounts of stuffing into the tight corners first – arms, legs, tail and muzzle. Gradually fill the rest of the body until the stuffing is firm and even, but not too tight.

9 Hand sew stuffing opening closed using a ladder stitch.

10 For the eyes, sew each black felt oval onto a white felt circle and then position the eyes on the head as marked. Sew in place. Make a French knot with white embroidery thread for each pupil, as marked on the pattern. Use 3 strands of black embroidery thread to sew a nose onto the muzzle using satin stitch. Then use 3 strands of pink embroidery thread to sew on the mouth using back stitch.

{kangaroo}

11 For each ear, pin together a solid colour fabric piece, patterned fabric piece and interfacing (with fabrics right sides facing). Sew together, leaving the base open for turning right side out. Turn right side out and iron flat. Turn the base edge of the ears under 6 mm (¼ in) and sew closed using a ladder stitch. Sew right and left bottom corners of the ear together to form a ring. Position ears on the head (y to y) and attach with a ladder stitch.

Joey finger puppet

MATERIALS

- Fabric – a scrap of plain fabric for the main body, lining, arms and ears; a scrap of new or vintage patterned fabric for the inner body.

INSTRUCTIONS

1 Trace and cut out the pattern using the template provided. Pin it to the fabric and cut out the pieces. You will need to cut 1 main body shape (cut on the fold), 1 lining shape (cut on the fold), 1 inner body shape, 4 arm shapes and 4 ear shapes from your fabric.

2 Fold the main body shape in half (right sides facing) and sew around the head from E to F.

3 Pin the inner body piece to the main body piece, right sides facing (E to E). Sew together, leaving the base open. Turn right side out and iron. Use a stuffing stick to firmly stuff the head and muzzle.

4 For the face, use 3 strands of black embroidery thread to make French knots for the eyes. Then satin stitch a nose. For the mouth, use 2 strands of pink embroidery thread and a back stitch.

5 Fold the lining piece in half (right sides facing) and sew together, leaving the base open. With right sides of the lining piece still facing, insert lining into the main body piece, so that the bottom edges of each line up. Turn the edge of the main body piece and the edge of the lining piece 6 mm (¼ in) under so that they are facing each other and use a ladder stitch to sew together.

6 For each ear and arm, pin 2 pieces together (right sides facing), and sew, leaving the base open for turning right side out. Turn right side out (use tweezers if necessary) and iron flat. Turn the base edge under 6 mm (¼ in) and sew closed using a ladder stitch. Sew right and left bottom corners of each ear together to form a ring. Position ears on the head (z to z) and arms on the body (o to o), and attach with a ladder stitch.

{CONTINUED}

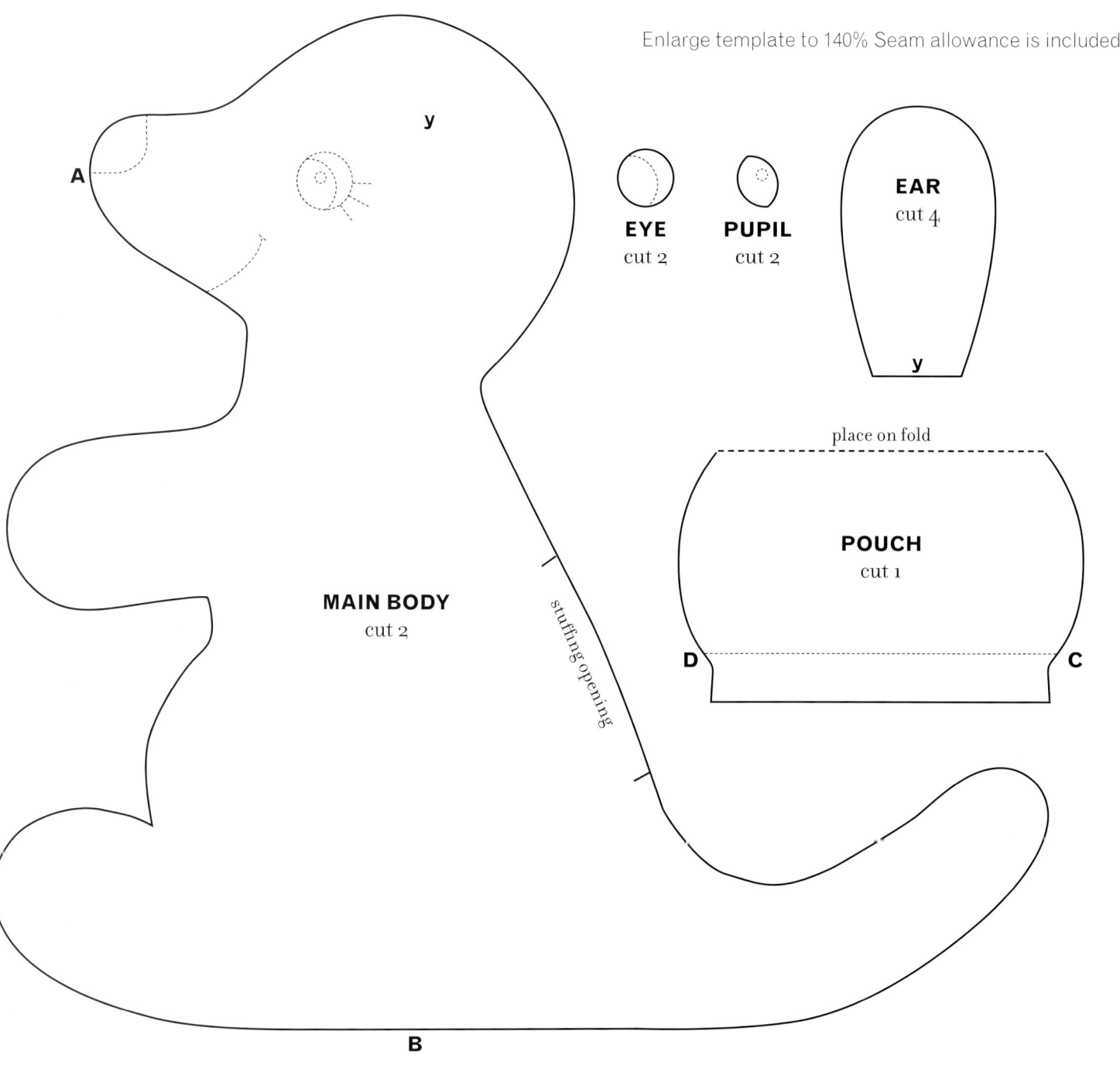

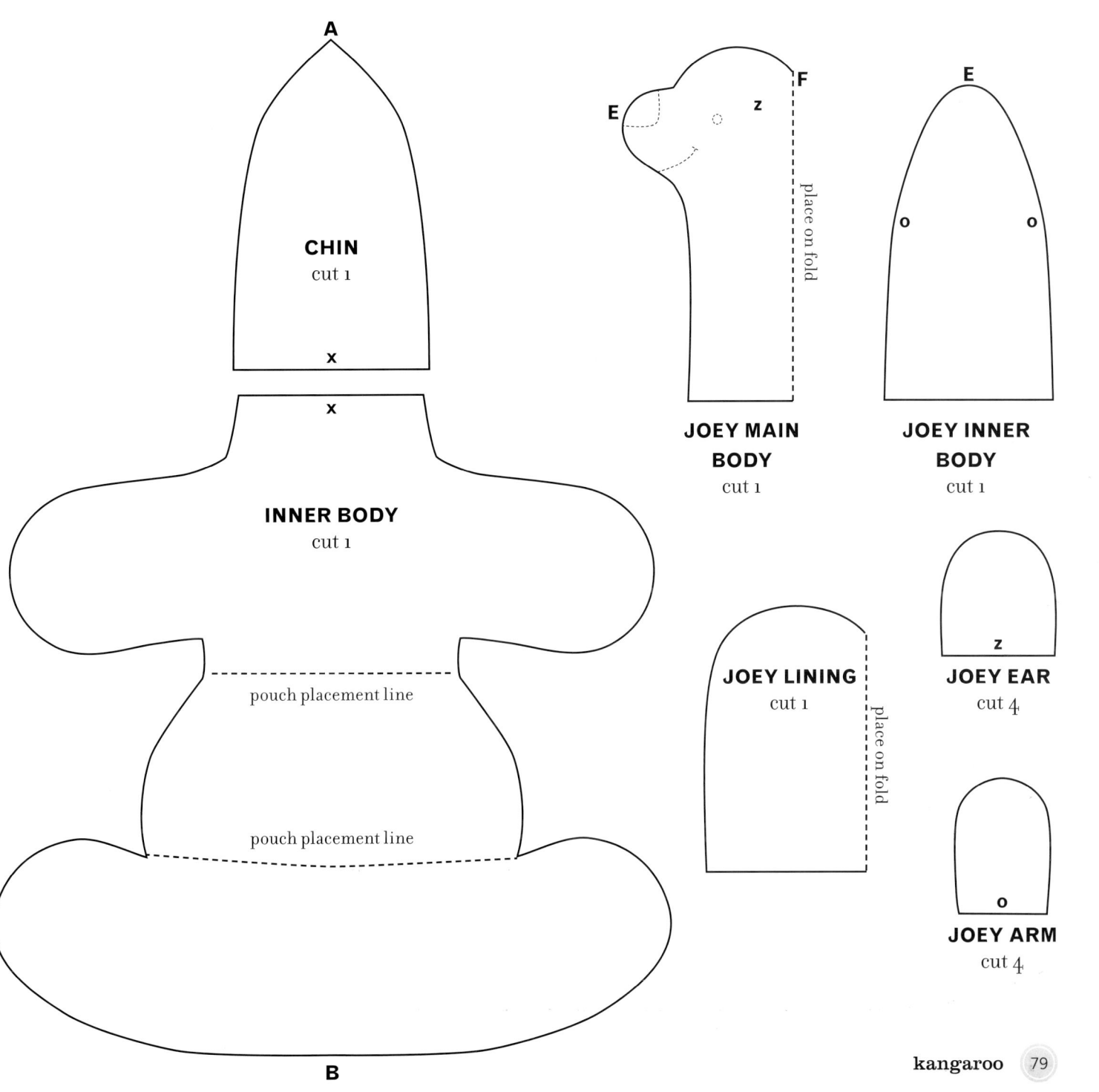

kangaroo

blossom bunny

{redfeltflower.blogspot.com} SARAH BOWE

Inspired by the simplicity of Japanese design, this bunny is made using a combination of linen, denim, felt and patterned fabric.

FINISHED SIZE
29 cm × 6 cm (11½ in × 2 in)

TOOLS
- Tracing paper
- Scissors
- Pins
- Sewing needle
- Sewing machine
- Iron
- Stuffing stick (or chopstick or pencil)

MATERIALS
- Body fabric – an 11 cm × 18 cm (4 in × 7 in) piece of linen for the head; a 9 cm × 18 cm (3½ in × 7 in) piece of patterned fabric for the upper body; a 9 cm × 18 cm (3½ in × 7 in) piece of denim for the lower body.
- Extra fabric – scraps of denim for the ears and a scrap of cream felt for the base.
- Thread – embroidery thread in 2 colours (light chocolate brown for the face; cream or beige for the ears and base); sewing thread to match body fabric.
- Decorations – two small beads for eyes (if the doll is for children over the age of 3, otherwise use French knots).
- Stuffing – polyfill; plastic beads or rice to weight base if required.

{CONTINUED}

{blossom bunny}

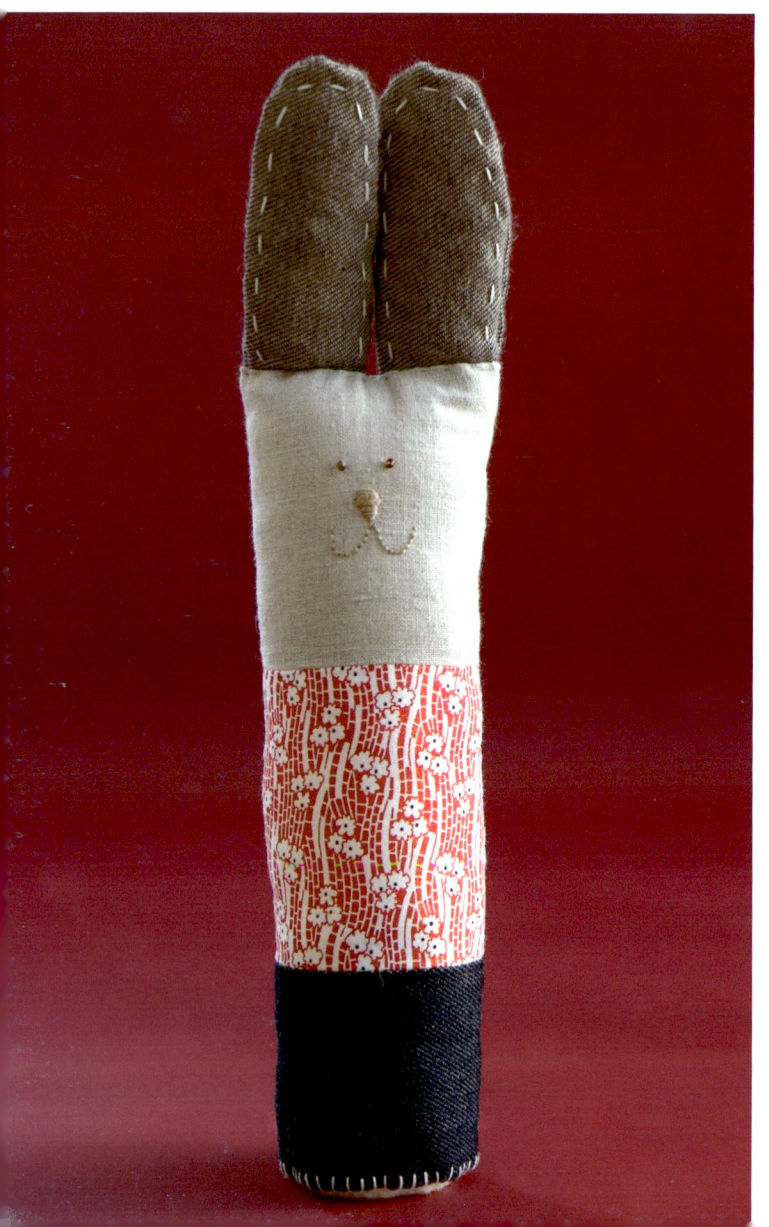

INSTRUCTIONS

1 Trace and cut out the enlarged pattern using the template provided. Pin it to the appropriate fabric and cut out the pieces. You will need to cut 1 head shape, 2 body shapes (1 in patterned fabric, 1 in denim), 1 base shape and 4 ear shapes from your fabric.

2 Pin head piece and patterned body piece together (right sides facing), and machine stitch along one long edge.

3 Pin patterned and denim body pieces together (right sides facing), and machine stitch along the edge. Iron all seams flat.

4 Embroider the nose and mouth onto the face, using 3 strands of light brown embroidery thread (as shown

{blossom bunny}

on the pattern). Use satin stitch for the nose and back stitch for the mouth. Sew on small beads for eyes (or use French knots if the toy is for a child under the age of 3).

5 With panels running horizontally, fold the stitched fabric in half (right sides facing) and machine stitch along the long edge, leaving a 10 mm (⅖ in) seam allowance. Fold over 2 cm (¾ in) at the top and 2 cm (¾ in) at the bottom (wrong sides facing) and press flat with the iron. Turn right side out.

6 For each of the ears, pin 2 pieces together (right sides facing) and machine stitch around the edge, leaving the base open. Turn right side out and embroider around the edge of the ear by hand with running stitch, using 3 strands of the cream embroidery thread. Use a stuffing stick to stuff ears with a small amount of polyfill.

7 Pin the ears to the top of the head (x to x), with the base of the ears about 6 mm (¼ in) inside the body. Use a slip stitch to attach the ears and sew up the top of the head.

8 Using a stuffing stick, stuff the body with polyfill.

9 If you want to weight the base, insert a small pouch of plastic beads or rice into the lower body section and surround with polyfill.

10 Tuck felt base piece into the lower body and secure to the denim with blanket stitch, using 3 strands of cream embroidery thread.

(CONTINUED)

Template shown at 100% Seam allowance is included

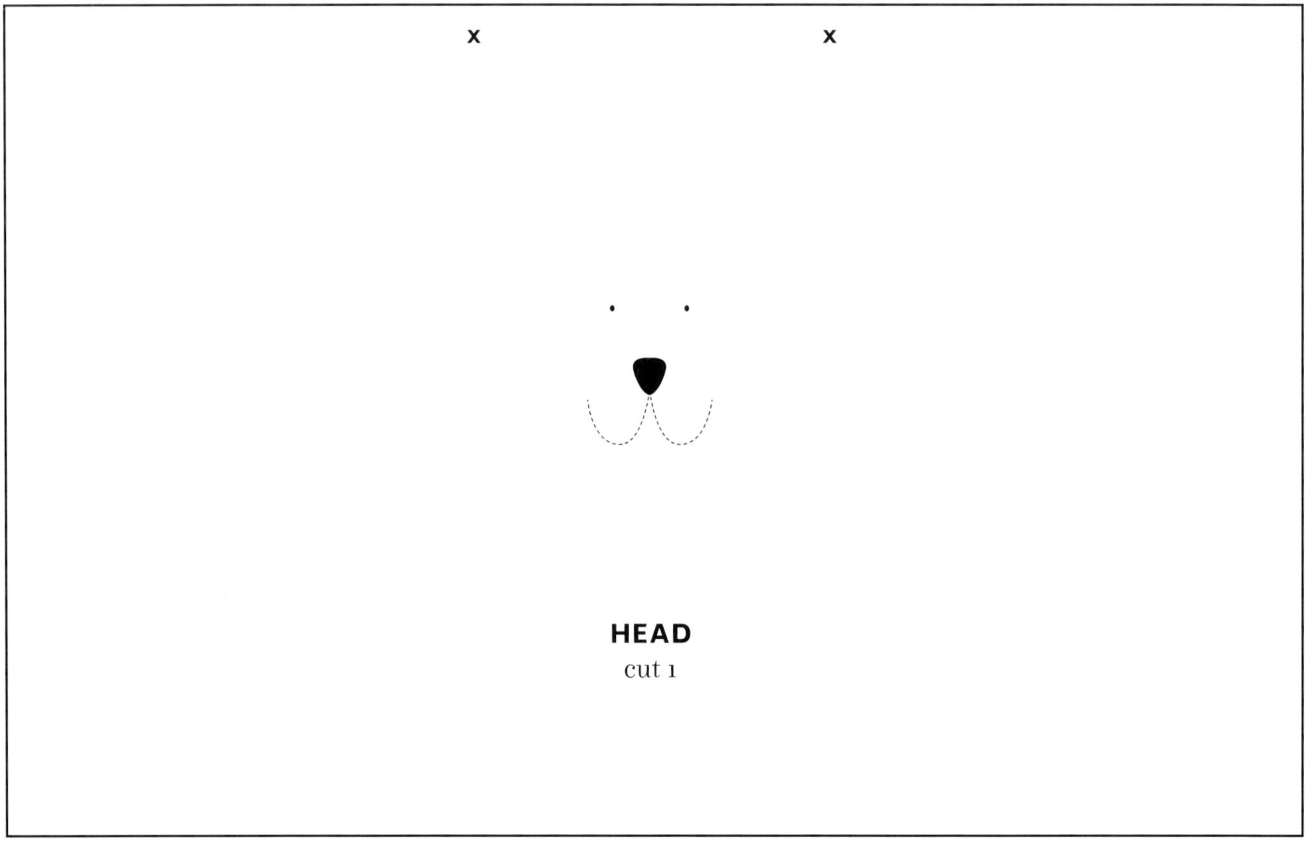

x   x

HEAD
cut 1

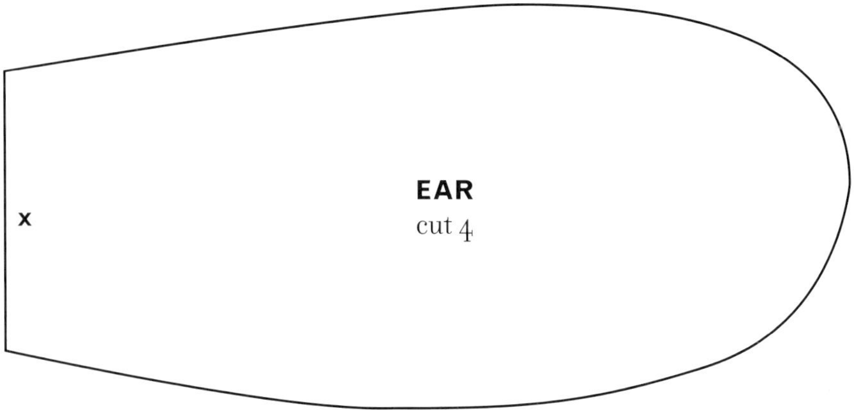

EAR
cut 4

84 blossom bunny

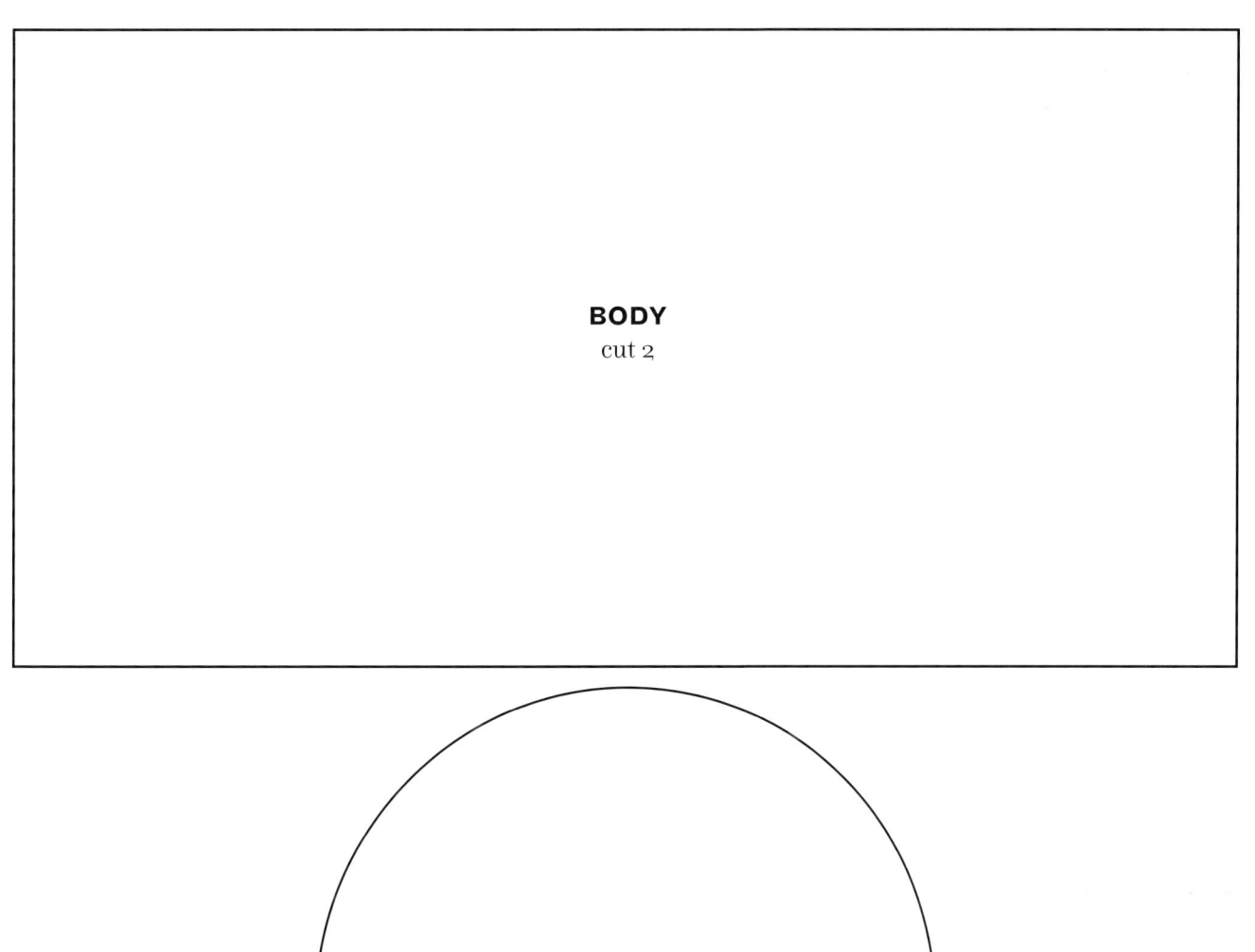

blossom bunny

pirate

{amysbabies.blogspot.com} AMY SHIMEL

Pirates have always been an obsession of mine – their freedom, charisma and adventurous spirit appeal to me on a deep, indefinable level. So when I started creating crochet dolls, designing a pirate was at the top of my list. Weeks of thought were followed by days of neglected housework, sore fingers and late nights, until finally my pirate doll was complete! (Note that this is an advanced crochet pattern.)

FINISHED SIZE
30 cm × 8 cm (12 in × 3 in) – excluding arms

TOOLS
- Crochet hooks: 1 × 3.5 mm (size E/4) and 1 × 1.8 mm (6 steel)
- Tapestry needle
- Serrated knife or small saw
- Sandpaper
- Sewing needle
- Stuffing stick (or chopstick or pencil)

MATERIALS
- **YARN**
  Dark-brown: 29 metres (26 yards) – boots and belt.
  Bone or tan: 54 metres (49 yards) – skin.
  Medium blue: 31 metres (28 yards) – pants.
  Dark-blue: 23 metres (21 yards) – vest.
  White: 31 metres (28 yards) – shirt.
  Off-white: 9 metres (8 yards) – sash.
  Dark-red: 6 metres (5 yards) – sash.
  Black: 116 metres (106 yards) – hair.
  Silver/grey: small amount of split-down yarn or embroidery thread of similar thickness – belt buckle.
- **SEWING THREAD**
  Black: to sew on eyes.
- **EMBROIDERY THREAD**
  Black: 13 skeins – hair.
  Dark-brown: 12 skeins – hair.
  Red: 3 skeins – headband.
- **DECORATIONS** – two small buttons for eyes. About 24 mixed vintage coloured beads, size 6/0 E (3.3 mm) (a combination of metal, wood and glass beads works nicely). About 30 clear iridescent beads, size 10/0 (2 mm). 1 × bamboo skewer.
- **STUFFING** – polyfill.

(CONTINUED)

{pirate}

ABBREVIATIONS

- **ch**   chain
- **sl st**   slip stitch
- **dc**   double crochet (**sc** single crochet in the US)
- **tr**   treble crochet (**dc** double crochet in the US)
- **htr**   half treble crochet (**hdc** half double crochet in the US)
- **dc dec**   decrease one stitch with double crochet (**sc dec** decrease one stitch with single crochet in the US)
- **sl st dec**   decrease one stitch with slip stitch
- **YOH**   yarn over hook (**YO** yarn over in the US)
- *****   indicates beginning of a section to be repeated

NOTES

There are several places in this pattern where you will be required to split the yarn and use only 2 ply instead of the standard 4 ply. Splitting is easiest with lengths about 5 metres long.

The doll is worked in the round unless otherwise instructed. Mark the last stitch in each round to keep track of where you are supposed to stop each round. This doll is crocheted with very tight tension (gauge) – tension is 6 stitches and 6 rows per 2.5 cm (1 in). Tight tension will stop the stuffing from showing through the stitches and help the doll keep its shape.

Some parts of this doll are started using the magic ring technique. Here are directions if you are unfamiliar with it.

1 Make a large loop by putting the yarn tail behind the working yarn (the yarn coming from the skein), leaving at least a 15 cm (6 in) tail until you become familiar with this method. Later, you may leave a shorter tail if desired.

2 With your hook, draw the working yarn through the loop, so you have one loop on the hook. (How you hold the loop while you work the stitches into it is personal preference, but some people find it convenient to put both their pinky and ring finger inside the loop to hold it tight.)

3 Treble crochet into the loop, crocheting over the tail. Continue to work as many trs as needed for your pattern into the loop. (Don't forget to keep crocheting over the tail.) When you are finished working stitches into the loop, you will likely find that the tail has curled around the loop a few times. To make it easier to draw the loop

{pirate}

closed, first untwist the tail, then pull the tail to draw the loop closed. You can leave an open hole in the center or draw it closed very tightly.

INSTRUCTIONS

1 HEAD

With black yarn:

R1 6 dc into the ring and pull the ring tight. Mark the last stitch. (6 dc.)

R2 2 dc into each stitch around. (12 dc.)

R3 *1 dc into the first stitch, 2 dc into next stitch, repeat from * to end. (18 dc.)

R4 *1 dc into each of the next 2 stitches, 2 dc into the next stitch, repeat from * to end. (24 dc.)

R5 *1 dc into each of the next 3 stitches, 2 dc into the next stitch, repeat from * to end. (30 dc.)

R6 *1 dc into each of the next 4 stitches, 2 dc into the next stitch, repeat from * to end. (36 dc.)

R7 *1 dc into each of the next 5 stitches, 2 dc into the next stitch, repeat from * to end. (42 dc.)

R8 *1 dc into each of the next 6 stitches, 2 dc into the next stitch, repeat from * to end. (48 stitches.)

R9 *1 dc into each of the next 7 stitches, 2 dc into the next stitch, repeat from * to end. (54 dc.)

Switch to tan yarn:

R10–17 dc into each stitch around. (54 dc.)

R18 *7 dc into next 7 stitches, dc dec, repeat from * to end. (48 dc.)

R19 *6 dc into next 6 stitches, dc dec, repeat from * to end. (42 dc.)

R20 *5 dc into next 5 stitches, dc dec, repeat from * to end. (36 dc.)

R21 *4 dc into next 4 stitches, dc dec, repeat from * to end. (30 dc.)

R22 *3 dc into next 3 stitches, dc dec, repeat from * to end. (24 dc.)

R23 *2 dc into next 2 stitches, dc dec, repeat from * to end. (18 dc.)

Finish off and leave a tail long enough to sew the head onto the body.

2 BOOTS

With dark-brown yarn:

R1 6 dc into the ring and pull the ring tight. Mark the last stitch. (6 dc.)

R2 2 dc into each stitch around. (12 dc.)

{CONTINUED}

{pirate}

R3 *1 dc into each of the next 3 stitches, 2 dc into the next stitch, repeat from * to end. (15 dc.)
R4–6 dc into each stitch around. (15 dc.)
R7 3 sl st, sl st dec, 2 sl st, 1 dc, dc dec, 3 dc, dc dec. (6 sl st, 6 dc.)
R8 6 dc into front loops, 6 dc into both loops. (12 dc.)
R9 *4 dc, dc dec, repeat from * to end. (10 dc.)
R10–18 dc into each stitch around. (10 dc.)

Put a small piece of stuffing into the leg and use a stuffing stick to push it towards the back of the foot to create the heel.

Switch to medium blue yarn:
R19 in back loops only, dc into each stitch around. (10 dc.)
R20 in both loops, *1 dc into each of the next 4 stitches, 2 dc into the next stitch, repeat from * to end. (12 dc.)
R21–26 dc into each stitch around. (12 dc.)
R27 1 dc into each of the next 5 stitches, 2 dc into the next stitch, repeat from * to end. (14 dc.)
R28–29 dc into each stitch around. (14 dc.)
R30 *1 dc into each of the next 6 stitches, 2 dc into the next stitch, repeat from * to end. (16 dc.)
R31–32 dc into each stitch around. (16 dc.)
R33 *1 dc into each of the next 7 stitches, 2 dc into the next stitch, repeat from * to end. (18 dc.)
R34–35 dc into each stitch around. (18 dc.)
R36 *1 dc into each of the next 8 stitches, 2 dc into the next stitch, repeat from * to end. (20 dc.)
R37 *1 dc into each of the next 9 stitches, 2 dc into the next stitch, repeat from * to end. (22 dc.)

Finish off. Use a stuffing stick to push the stuffing down to the tip of the boot.

3 BOOT CUFF

This will require you to split your yarn from 4 ply to 2 ply. Crochet using the same tension as the rest of the doll. This will make the cuff stiff and it will hold its shape.

With dark-brown 2-ply yarn:
Go back to the front loops you missed when connecting the blue pant leg to the brown boot. Connect your yarn with a sl st to the first missed loop.

R1 dc into the same loop and into each loop around.
R2 *1 dc into each of the next 4 stitches, 2 dc into the next loop, repeat from * to end. (12 dc.)
R3 *1 dc into each of the next 5 stitches, 2 dc into the next stitch, repeat from * to end. (14 dc.)
R4 *1 dc into each of the next 6 stitches, 2 dc into the

{pirate}

next stitch, repeat from * to end. (16 dc.)

R5 * 1 dc into each of the next 7 stitches, 2 dc into the next stitch, repeat from * to end. (18 dc.)

R6 *1 dc into each of the next 8 stitches, 2 dc into the next stitch, repeat from * to end. (20 dc.)

R7 *1 dc into each of the next 9 stitches, 2 dc into the next stitch, repeat from * to end. (22 dc.)

R8–10 dc into each stitch around. (22 dc.)

Finish off and weave in the end with the tapestry needle. Fold down cuff.

4 TORSO

The legs have 22 stitches in them at the top. Two of those stitches on each leg will only be used to create the crotch area and then will be missed to create the rest of the torso. Align the 2 crotch stitches on the legs. Attach medium-blue colour with a sl st through both legs. Sl st into the next stitch through both legs creating the crotch. Miss these two sl st from now on.

With medium-blue yarn:

R1 20 dc onto the first leg, 20 dc onto the second leg. (40 dc.)

R2–7 dc into each stitch around. (40 dc.)

R8 *8 dc, dc dec, repeat from * 4 times. (36 dc.)

Switch to white yarn (you will also be using the tan, so do not tie off the colours until instructed):

R9–15 dc into each stitch around. (36 dc.)

R16 with white 2 dc, with tan 2 dc, with white 32 dc.

R17 with white 2 dc, with tan 3 dc, with white 31 dc.

R18 with white 2 dc, with tan 4 dc, with white 30 dc.

R19 with white 2 dc, with tan 5 dc, with white 29 dc.

R20 with white 2 dc, with tan 6 dc, with white 28 dc.

R21 with white 2 dc, with tan 7 dc, with white 27 dc.

R22 with white 2 dc, with tan 8 dc, with white 26 dc.

R23 with white 2 dc, with tan 2dc, dc dec, 4dc, with white dc dec, *4dc, dc dec, repeat from * 4 times. (30 stitches.)

R24 with white 2 dc, with tan 1 dc, dc dec, 3dc, dc dec, with white *3dc, dc dec, repeat from * 4 times. (24 stitches.)

Switch to tan yarn:

R25 *2 dc, dc dec, repeat from * to end. (18 dc.)

R26–27 dc into each stitch around. (18 dc.)

Finish off and use a stuffing stick to stuff the torso up to the top of the neck.

{CONTINUED}

{pirate}

5 ARMS

Fingers on the hands are made with a double treble crochet bobble. The bobble is made in the following way.

With tan yarn:
*YOH twice, insert into stitch indicated. YOH again and draw up a loop. YOH and draw through loop (twice). Repeat from * twice, leaving 4 loops total on the hook. YOH one last time and draw it through all 4 loops. Continue stitching as pattern indicates.

With tan yarn:
- **R1** 6 dc into the loop and pull the loop tight. Mark the last stitch.
- **R2** 2 dc into next stitch, *1 dc, 1 bobble in the same stitch, repeat from * 3 times, 2 dc into each of next 2 dc. (12 stitches.)
- **R3–4** dc into each stitch around. (12 dc.)
- **R5** For right hand: 3 dc, 1 bobble for thumb, 8 dc. For left hand: 9 dc, 1 bobble for thumb, 2 dc.
- **R6** *4 dc, dc dec, repeat from * twice. (10 dc.)
- **R7** *3 dc, dc dec, repeat from * twice. (8 dc.)
- **R8–30** dc into each stitch around. (8 dc.)

Finish off. Shape the hand by pressing it around your thumb to give the palm a curve.

6 SHIRT SLEEVES

This will require you to split your yarn from 4 ply to 2 ply. Crochet this part in a slightly looser tension to make the fabric softer. Leave a long tail at the beginning that will be used to sew the sleeve to the arm and then the sleeve/arm to the torso.

With white yarn:
Using 2 ply, ch 10.
- **R1** connect to first chain with a sl st to form a ring. 20 dc into the ring. (20 dc.)
- **R2–30** dc into each stitch around. (20 dc, 1 turning chain.)

The rest of the sleeve is worked in rows, not rounds:

- **R31** ch 1 and turn. Dc in each stitch across. Ch 1 and turn. (20 dc, 1 turning chain.)
- **R32–35** dc into each stitch across. Ch 1 and turn. (20 dc.)
- **R36** dc dec across 10 times. (10 dc.)
- **R37–39** dc into each stitch across. (10 dc.)

{pirate}

Finish off and weave in end with tapestry needle. Put the arms in the sleeves. The sleeves should come down over the hands. Using the long tail left at the top of the sleeve, sew the first row of the sleeve to the first row of the arm. Using the same piece of yarn, sew the arm and sleeve to the torso two rounds below the neck colour change. The sleeve on the doll's left arm should be left open and should cover the hand. The sleeve on the doll's right arm should have the cuff sewn shut over the wrist and the extra length should pouf around the cuff.

7 VEST

The vest is worked in 3 pieces and sewn together at the shoulder and side/back seams. It is worked in rows instead of rounds. It will require you to split your yarn from 4 ply to 2 ply. Crochet this part in a slightly looser tension to make the fabric softer. Leave a long tail at the beginning of the front pieces that will be used to sew the shoulder seams. Make 2 front pieces and one back. All the pieces are worked from the top to the bottom. The front pieces will be longer than the back.

With dark-blue yarn, for the vest front:
Using 2 ply, ch 5.

R1 miss the first chain after the hook and dc into each of the other chains. Ch 1 and turn. (4dc.)
R2–7 dc into each stitch across. Ch 1 and turn. (4 dc.)
R8 dc into each stitch across. Ch 4 and turn. (4 dc/4 ch.)
R9 miss the first chain after the hook. 3 dc into chains, 4 dc into the remaining stitches. Ch 1 and turn. (7 dc.)
R10 dc into each stitch across. Ch 4 and turn. (7 dc/4 ch.)
R11 miss the first chain after the hook. 3 dc into chains, 7 dc into the remaining stitches. Ch 1 and turn. (10 dc.)
R12–41 dc into each stitch across. Ch 1 and turn. (10 dc.)

Finish off and weave in the end.

With dark-blue yarn, for the vest back:
Using 2 ply, ch 16.
R1 miss the first chain after the hook and dc into each of the other chains. Ch 1 and turn. (15 dc.)
R2–19 dc into each stitch across. Ch 1 and turn. (15 dc.)

Finish off and weave in the end.

To put the vest pieces together, line up the top of the shoulder with the first 4 ch on each side of the top edge of the back and sew them together. Finish off and weave in ends. Count down the back 6 rows. This will be where you begin to sew the back side seams. Sew them

{CONTINUED}

{pirate}

all the way to the bottom of the back. Finish off and weave in ends. Put vest on the doll.

8 SASH

This will alternate between off-white and dark-red yarn. It will require you to split your yarn from 4 ply to 2 ply. Crochet this part in a slightly looser tension to make the fabric softer. The sash will be long enough to go around the waist (where the blue and white meet) with some left over to hang down the sides. Do not weave in the ends; this will give the sash a frayed look. The ends should be about 2.5 cm (1 in) long. This piece is worked in rows instead of rounds.

With off-white and dark-red yarn:
Using the off-white and leaving a tail about 2.5 cm (1 in) long, ch 76.

R1 miss the first chain after the hook and dc into each stitch across. Tie off and leave a tail about 2.5 cm (1 in) long. (75 dc.)

R2 turn. Using the dark-red and leaving a 2.5 cm (1 in) tail, attach the yarn with a sl st to the first chain. Dc into the same stitch and into each stitch across. Tie off and leave a tail about 2.5 cm (1 in) long. (75 dc.)

R3 turn. Using the off-white and leaving 2.5 cm (1 in) tail, attach the yarn with a sl st to the first chain. Dc into the same stitch and into each stitch across. Ch 1 and turn. (75 dc.)

R4 dc into each stitch across. Tie off and leave a 2.5 cm (1 in) tail. (75 dc.)

R5 turn. Using the dark-red and leaving a 2.5 cm (1 in) tail, attach the yarn with a sl st to the first chain. Dc into the same stitch and into each stitch across. Tie off and leave a tail about 2.5 cm (1 in) long. (75 dc.)

R6 turn. Using the off-white and leaving a 2.5 cm (1 in) tail, attach the yarn with a sl st to the first chain. Dc into the same stitch and into each stitch across. Ch 1 and turn. (75 dc.)

R7 dc into each stitch across. Tie off and leave a 2.5 cm (1 in) tail. (75 dc.)

Wrap the sash around the doll over the vest. On the doll's left side, tie it with a simple overlap leaving one end longer than the other. This extra end will be folded with part above the belt and part below. Use a pin to hold the sash in place while you are putting the belt on the doll. The belt will hold the sash in place.

{pirate}

9 BELT

The belt is made with the small steel hook. It is worked in rows instead of rounds. It will require you to split your yarn from 4 ply to 2 ply. Crochet this part in a tight tension so it holds its shape.

With dark-brown yarn:
Using 2 ply, ch 86.
R1 miss the first chain after the hook and dc into each of the other chains across. (85 dc.)

Finish off and weave in end.

10 BELT BUCKLE

With silver/grey yarn or embroidery thread:
R1 attach to the end of the belt with a sl st. Sl st into the same stitch. Ch 4. Dc into the bottom loop of the same stitch. Ch 1 and turn.
R2 6 dc into the loop created in the previous row.

Finish off and weave in. Wrap belt around the doll with the belt buckle coming from the doll's left side. Put the other end of the belt through the buckle and pull it tight. Centre the buckle on the doll. To tie the knot to hold the belt, take the end of the belt and fold it back the direction it came from. Put the end under the belt from the bottom up, keeping a loop. Take the end and put it down through the loop and pull tight.

11 HEADBAND

The headband is made with the small steel hook. It is worked in rows instead of rounds. Crochet this part in a tight tension so it holds its shape.

With red embroidery thread:
Ch 151.
R1 miss the first chain after the hook, 5 dc, 140 htr, 5 dc, turn.
R2 miss first dc after the hook, 4 sl st, 5 dc, 130 htr, 5 dc, turn.
R3 miss first sl st after the hook, 5 sl st, 5 dc, 120 htr, 5 dc, turn.
R4 miss first sl st after the hook, 5 sl st, 5 dc, 110 htr, 5 dc, turn.
R5 miss first sl st after the hook, 5 sl st, 5 dc, 100 htr, 5 dc.

{CONTINUED}

{pirate}

Finish off and weave in the ends.

12 At this point you should have an assembled body, a bald head and a headband. Decide where you want the face to be and sew on the buttons for eyes.

13 The next stage is to attach the hair. The hair will be held in with a knot on the inside of the head, and is woven into the head in a repeating pattern: 2 embroidery thread bundles, 1 yarn bundle. The first two rows have bundles worked into each hole to outline the hairline. The fill-in area is worked with a bundle in every other space, like a checker board. The hair will be very long at first, but will be cut to length at the end of the styling process.

To make the hair: cut 12 skeins of black and 12 skeins of brown embroidery thread into 50 cm (½ yard) pieces. Cut 192 x 50 cm (½ yard) pieces of black yarn. Take one black and one brown piece of embroidery thread and line them up together. Fold the threads in half, matching up the cut ends. Take this by the fold and tie a knot as close to the fold as possible. Do the same for all the rest of the embroidery thread pairs, then fold and knot the yarn in the same manner.

To weave the hair into the head, start at the hairline (where the black and tan meet).

Push the 3.5 mm (E/4) hook into one of the spaces on the black side of the line. Take one of the embroidery thread bunches and fold it over the hook. Pull the hook back up through the head with the hair on it. Be careful not to pull the knot through the head. Outline the brow and 7 rows down both sides of the face. Stop at the row before the decreases begin. Do a second outline row. Fill in the hair from the bottom up. Remember to work a bundle in every other space, like a checker board. When you get to the top you will begin to work in a spiral. The center of the head will be left empty. Use all the bundles.

14 Use a stuffing stick to stuff the head. Begin sewing the head to the body. Leave about 3 stitches undone and use the hole to stuff the neck. Finish sewing the neck shut. Using the leftover black skein of embroidery thread, stitch on the moustache and goatee. Cut 6 × 15 cm (6 in) pieces of embroidery thread for the beard. Using the tapestry needle, insert the embroidery thread in one space and out the other. Braid it and tie it off at about 4 cm (1½ in) long.

{pirate}

15 Separate the hair into 2 bunches: above the black/tan line and below the black/tan line. Tie the headband around this line. You will need to cut two lengths of embroidery thread for tying the braid and side ponytail. The side ponytail is made from the first row of hair across the brow only. Take this section of hair over to the right side of the head and tie it off. Break the rest of the brow hair into 3 pieces and begin to braid it in a loose French braid. Stop pulling up hair from the sides about half way to the back, finish off the braid and tie it off. The braid should be loose enough to cover the bald patch, but tight enough to hold together.

Cut the rest of the hair raggedly to about the same length as the finished braid; a little longer than shoulder length.

16 There are 3 beaded strands in the pirate's hair. To make these you will need a needle small enough to go through the beads but still hold 6 strands of black embroidery thread.

Use 5 of the vintage size 6/0 (3.3 mm) beads for the first (short) strand. Using 3 strands of black embroidery thread, string the beads, leaving a tail about 8 cm (3 in) long. Skipping the first bead after the needle, thread the needle back through the beads again. Use all 6 strands of embroidery thread to sew the strand to the inside of the headband, just over the inner edge of the right eye.

Use 9 of the vintage size 6/0 (3.3 mm) beads for the second (medium) strand. The beads are strung in the same manner as for the small strand. Sew the strand to the inside of the headband on the right side of his face.

The last (long) strand has a three-armed 'chandelier' on the bottom made of the smaller 10/0 (2 mm) beads. The rest of the strand is made of the remaining 10 vintage 6/0 (3.3 mm) beads. Thread the needle with 3 strands of black embroidery thread. String 10 of the smaller beads, leaving a long tail. Skipping the first bead after the needle, pass the needle back through the other beads. Repeat this process twice, leaving you with 3 strands of beads on the same length of embroidery thread. Move them close together and thread the needle with all 6 strands of thread. String the larger beads. Sew the strand to the inside of the headband on the left side of the face.

{pirate}

17 There are 2 pieces of bamboo in the pirate's hair, these are cut from the thick bamboo skewer. Each one should measure 5–8 cm (2–3 in) long. Measure and mark your skewer. Using a serrated knife or a small saw, cut the pieces from the skewer. Use sandpaper to shape and smooth the pieces.

Cut a very shallow groove around each piece of bamboo, near the top end. This groove will help hold the embroidery thread that will be wrapped around the pieces. Take a long piece of 3-strand embroidery thread and begin wrapping it around the bamboo where you cut the groove. Keep wrapping until you have about 6 mm (¼ in) of the top of the piece wrapped.

Put a needle on the end of the thread and put it through the wrapping 2 or 3 times to secure. Leave the embroidery thread long on this piece.

Repeat the wrapping process with the second piece of bamboo. After you thread through the wrapping on the second piece, position the pieces how you want them to be in the hair.

Thread through the wrapping of both pieces to hold them in place, and cut the embroidery thread. Using the thread that had been left long, wrap it between the two pieces several times to hold them and then tie it to the side ponytail. Any left over thread can be worked into the head hair and hidden.

Many thanks to Donna Hulka for permission to use her instructions for the magic ring technique (www.yarntomato.com).

beetle bug

{Nest Studio — neststudio.typepad.com} CARLY SCHWERDT

With her bold, simple design, this happy little bug will flit into your life and brighten up your day.

FINISHED SIZE
20 cm × 17 cm (8 in × 7 in)

TOOLS
- Tracing paper
- Scissors
- Pins
- Sewing needle
- Sewing machine
- Stuffing stick (or chopstick or pencil)

MATERIALS
- Body fabric – 2 fat quarters of patterned cotton fabric.
- Extra fabric – a scrap of blue or lilac felt for the wings; a fat quarter of striped fabric for the legs; a fat quarter of wool blanketing for the head; a scrap of wool felt in beige, cream or brown for the eyes.
- Thread – black sewing thread; brown and red embroidery thread for the face details.
- Stuffing – polyfill or wool rovings.

INSTRUCTIONS

1 Trace and cut out the pattern using the template provided. Pin it to the appropriate fabric and cut out the pieces. (I like to cut freehand without a pattern, as it makes for individual quirky toys – you can try this, using the pattern as a rough guide). You will need to cut 2 body shapes, 2 head shapes, 8 leg shapes, 2 wing shapes, and 1 of each eye shape from your fabric.

2 For each leg, pin 2 pieces together (right sides facing) and sew together with the sewing machine, leaving the ends open for turning right side out. Turn right side out. (I like the legs to be floppy, so I don't stuff them. If you prefer them firm, you'll need to stuff them now, before attaching them to the body.)

3 For the face, use the sewing thread to neatly sew the felt eyes to the right side of one of the woollen head pieces, as shown on the pattern. Embroider nose with brown embroidery thread, and sew a cross-stitch onto each eye. Use red embroidery thread for the mouth.

(CONTINUED)

{beetle bug}

4 Pin each head piece to a body piece, x to x, (right sides facing) and sew from A to B.

5 Pin the two wing pieces together (wrong sides facing) and use a running stitch to sew them together.

6 Place the front head/body piece right side up on your work surface. Pin the wings and legs into position (y to y and z to z), pointing in towards the body and remembering which way they will face when the body is turned right side out (see diagram on page 3) Place the second head/body piece right side down on top and pin pieces together. Sew, securing legs and wings in place as you go, and leaving an opening for turning right side out and stuffing (as marked). (I always double stitch over the wings and legs, to make them extra strong.)

7 Trim all edges, but leave at least a 10 mm (⅖ in) border. With scissors, clip fabric around the curved edges. Be careful not to clip the seam. Turn right side out (take your time, as this can be a bit tricky).

8 Using a stuffing stick, push small amounts of stuffing into the body until the stuffing is firm and even, but not too tight.

9 Hand sew the stuffing opening closed using a whip stitch.

{CONTINUED}

Template shown at 100% Seam allowance is included

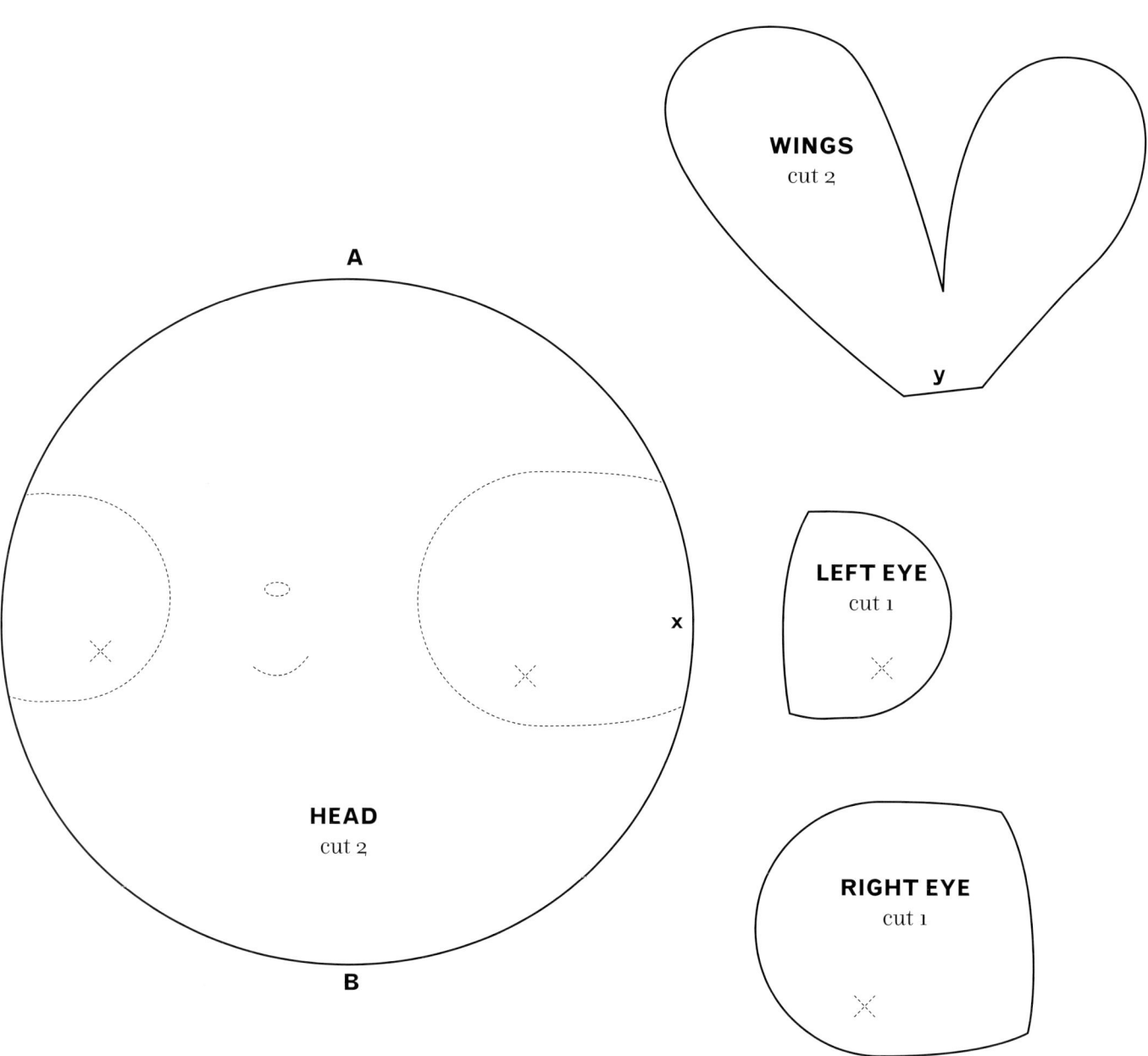

beetle bug

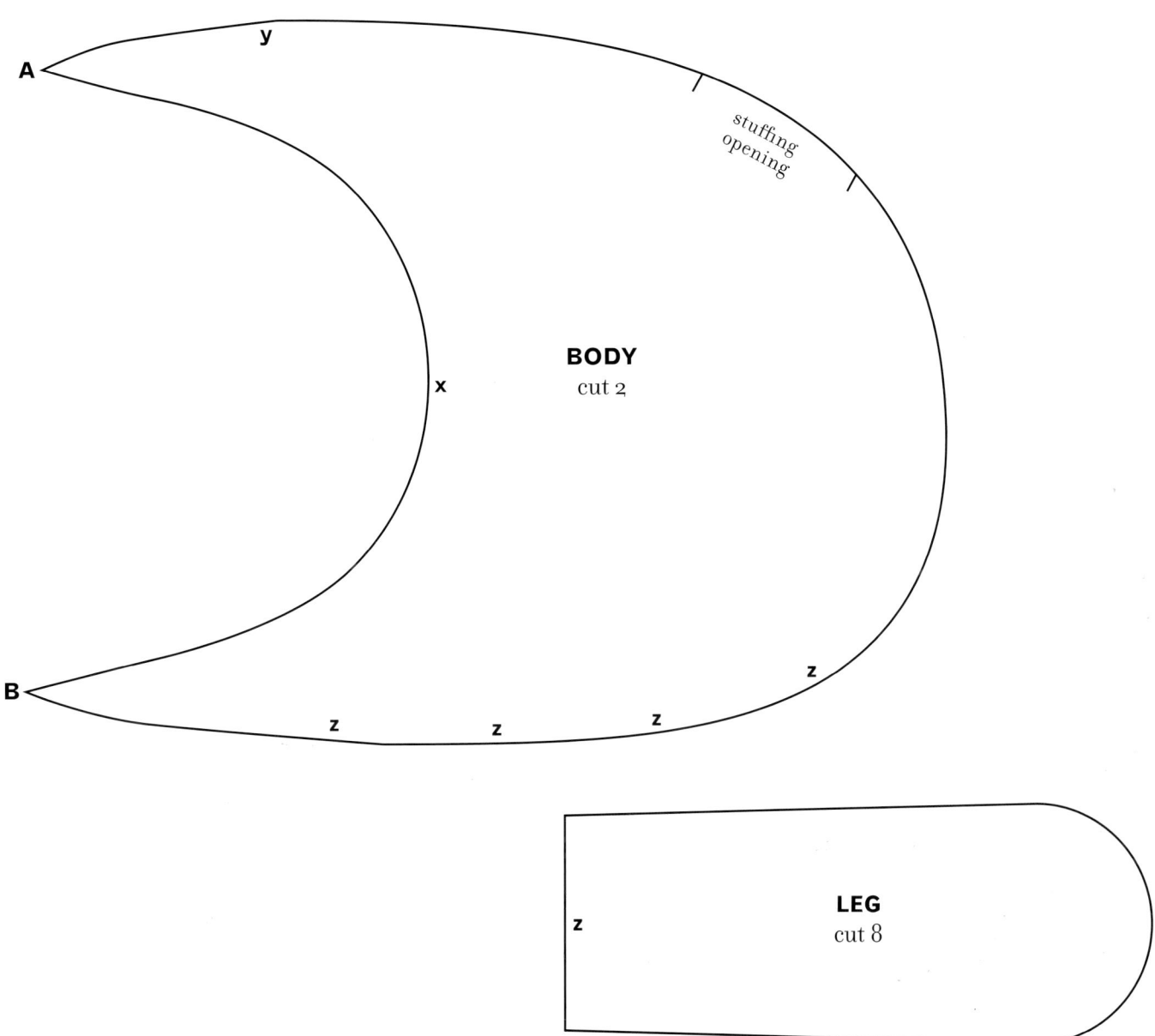

beetle bug 103

cat

{karkovski — www.karkovski.typepad.com} KRISTINA KARKOV THERKILDSEN

This cat is a twist on a pattern I made when I first began creating softies. The design is quite simple, but with some colourful vintage fabric, it really comes alive. Be sure to stuff the cat firmly for best results.

FINISHED SIZE
21 cm × 10 cm (8 in × 4 in)

TOOLS
- Tracing paper
- Scissors
- Pins
- Sewing needle and/or machine
- Stuffing stick (or chopstick or pencil)

MATERIALS
- Body fabric – a 20 cm × 50 cm (8 in × 20 in) piece of new or vintage fabric, either patterned or plain.
- Thread – coloured sewing thread to match the body fabric.
- Stuffing – polyfill and rice.

INSTRUCTIONS

1 Trace and cut out the enlarged pattern using the template provided. Pin it to the fabric and cut out the pieces. You will need to cut 2 body shapes and 1 bottom shape.

2 If you want to add any embellishments, such as face details, sew them on to one of the body pieces now.

3 Pin the two body pieces together (right sides facing), and sew. Leave a 4 cm (1½ in) opening for turning right side out and stuffing (as marked on the pattern). Leave the bottom open. Clip all curves close to the stitch line to allow for a smoother finish after turning right side out.

{CONTINUED}

{cat}

4 Pin bottom piece to body (right sides facing), and sew. Turn right side out.

5 Fill the bottom of the cat with rice.

6 Using a stuffing stick, push small amounts of stuffing into the ears and head. Stuff the rest of the body until the stuffing is very firm. Hand sew the stuffing opening closed using a whip stitch.

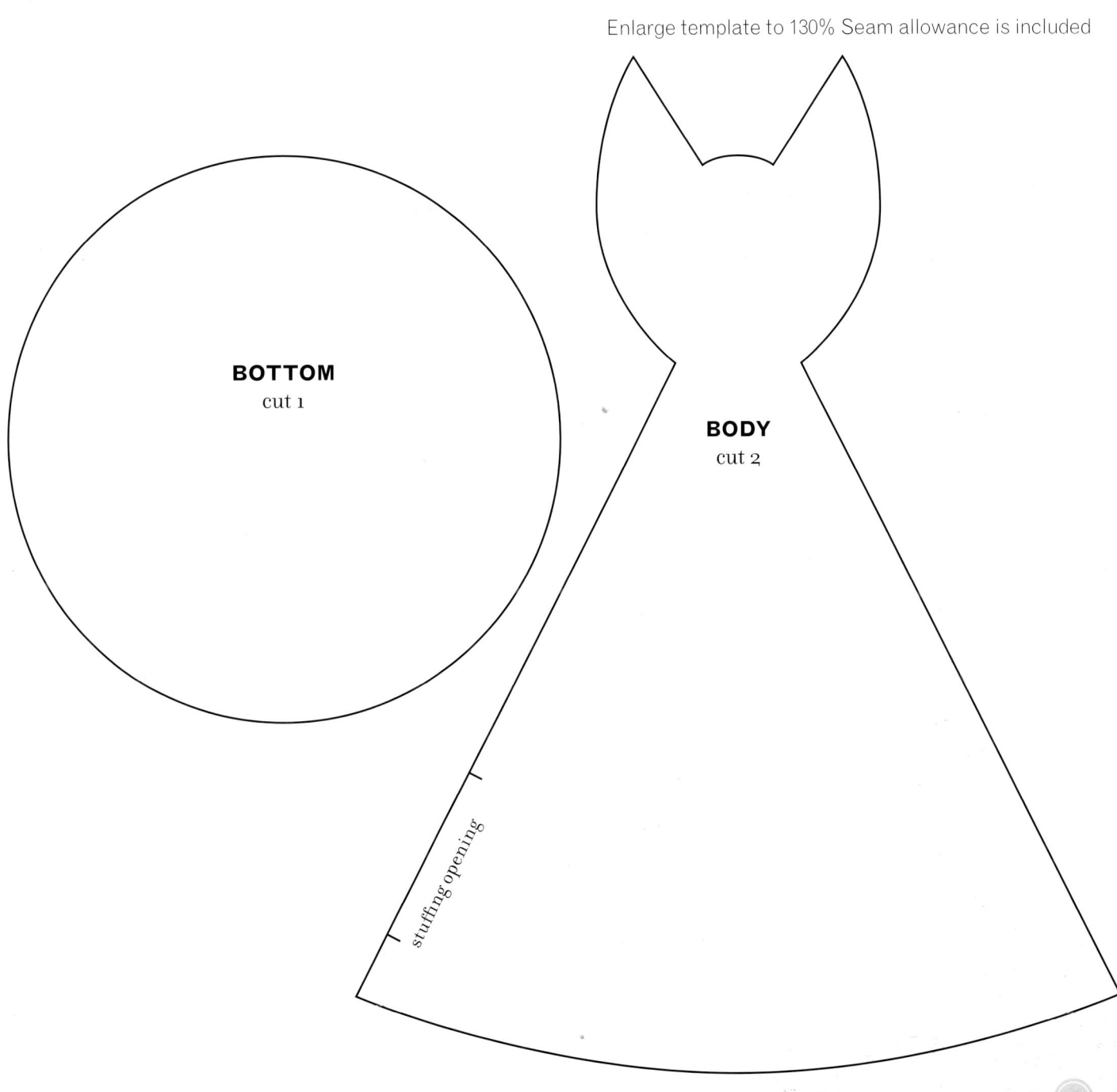

mad dog

{herzensart — www.herzensart.com} SANDRA MONAT

I think it's important to have a sense of humour and not take life too seriously sometimes. That's why I created this mad dog, as a homage to a friend's dog that is a little bit neurotic (although she's actually a good girl). This toy is suitable for beginners as it is very easy to make.

FINISHED SIZE
35 cm × 40 cm (14 in × 16 in)

TOOLS
- Tracing paper
- Scissors
- Pins
- Sewing needle
- Sewing machine
- Stuffing stick (or chopstick or pencil)

MATERIALS
- Body fabric — a 50 cm × 50 cm (20 in × 20 in) piece of strong fake-fur fabric.
- Extra fabric — a scrap of white felt for eyes and teeth.
- Thread — sewing thread to match body fabric; plus thick white thread for eyes and teeth.
- Decorations — a small red button for the eye.
- Stuffing — polyfill.

{CONTINUED}

{mad dog}

INSTRUCTIONS

1 Trace and cut out the enlarged pattern using the template provided. Pin it to the fabric and cut out the pieces. You will need to cut 2 body shapes, 1 eye ring and 1 teeth shape.

2 Pin the body pieces together (right sides facing) and sew, leaving an opening for turning right side out and stuffing, as shown on the pattern. With scissors, trim edges and clip fabric around the curves. Be careful not to clip the seam. Turn right side out.

3 Using a stuffing stick, push small amounts of stuffing into the tight corners first – ears, nose, legs and tail. Gradually fill the rest of the body until the stuffing is firm and even. Hand sew the stuffing opening closed.

4 Pin the eye-ring onto the face as marked on the pattern, and stitch on with white thread. Do the same with the teeth. Sew the red button into the centre of the eye ring. (Use red felt instead of a button if this toy is for a child under 3 years.)

5 Use thick white thread to make a large cross-stitch for the second eye (as marked), then repeat the stitch a few times until you have a thick cross. (Alternatively you could cut a cross out of white felt and sew it on.)

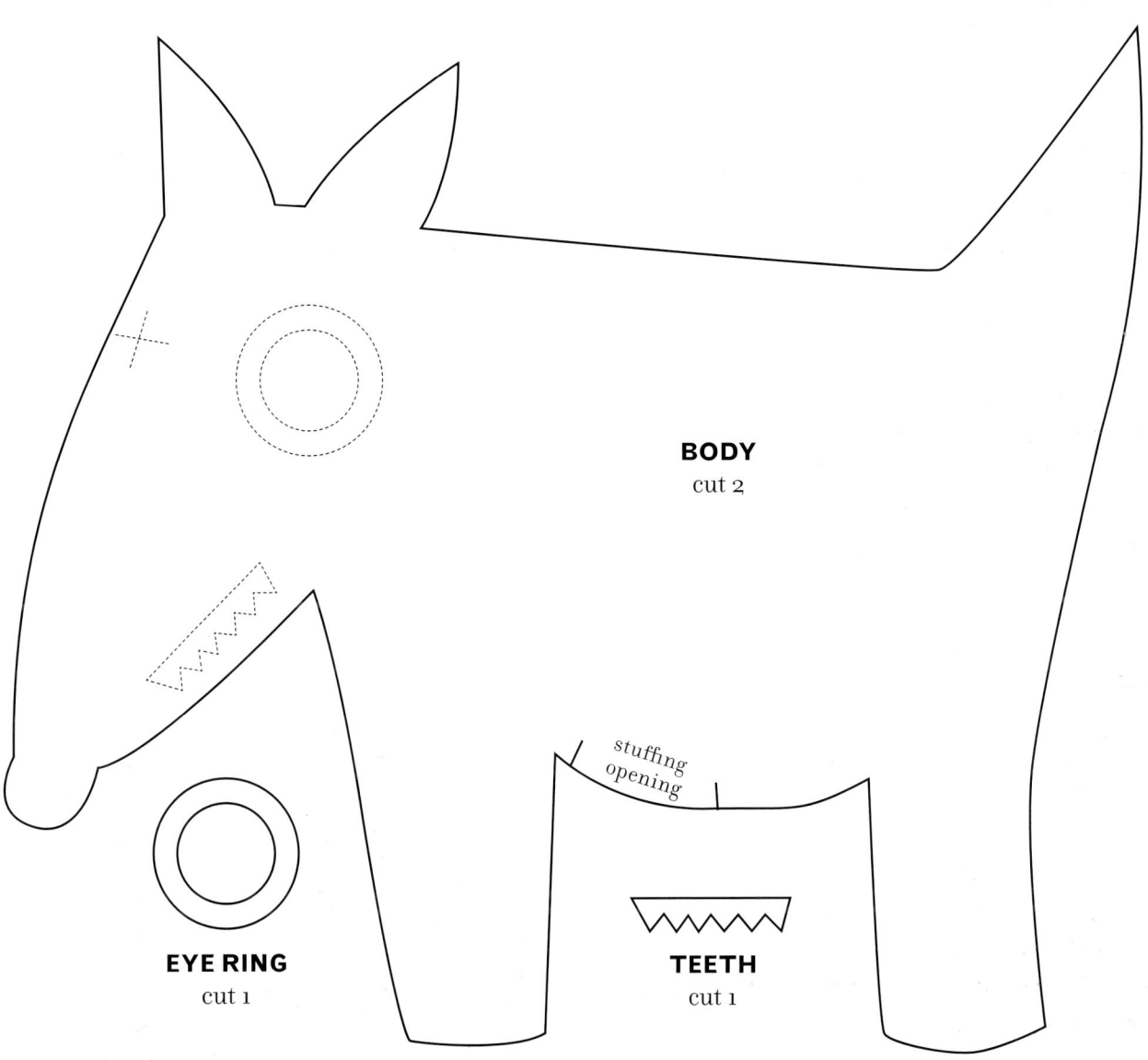

cosmonaut devil

{Bonspiel! – bonspielcreation.com} ELLEN BOX

It is very important to use a stretchy polar fleece fabric for this toy, in order to produce that flawless CGI-like surface. If you really get rolling and decide to make an army of these little devils, I guarantee you'll laugh your head off at the result.

FINISHED SIZE
30 cm × 15 cm (12 in × 6 in)

TOOLS
- Tracing paper
- Scissors
- Pins
- Sewing needle
- Sewing machine
- Stuffing stick and blunt pencil
- Tweezers

MATERIALS
- Body fabric – a 36 cm × 51 cm (14 in × 20 cm) piece of polar fleece or similar stretchy fabric.
- Extra fabric – a 10 cm × 12 cm (5 in × 4 in) piece of contrasting stretchy fabric for the face.
- Thread – sewing thread to match body fabric; embroidery thread in a contrasting colour for the mouth.
- Decorations – 2 buttons, doll eyes or home-made polymer clay eyes. (Tip: you can make the eyes shiny by applying clear nail polish.) 1 star appliqué (or make your own out of felt).
- Stuffing – polyfill.

(CONTINUED)

{cosmonaut devil}

INSTRUCTIONS

1 Trace and cut out the enlarged pattern using the template provided. Pin it to the fabric (with the stretch going horizontally) and cut out the pieces. You will need to cut 2 body shapes, 2 foot shapes, 1 square face shape, 1 star shape (if using) and 4 horn shapes from your fabric. Cut the oval face shape out of one of the body pieces to leave a hole (as marked) – you can discard the piece you've removed.

2 Place the square face piece behind the oval face opening on the front body piece and pin in place. Stitch on, sewing very close to the edge of the opening.

3 Sew the eyes onto the face and embroider the mouth. Sew the star shape or appliqué onto the front body piece as marked.

{cosmonaut devil}

4 For each horn, pin 2 pieces together (right sides facing) and sew, leaving the bottom open. Trim edges. Turn right side out using tweezers. Use the point of a blunt pencil to gently push a small amount of stuffing right to the end of the horn, so that it forms a point.

5 Place the front body piece right side up on your work surface. Pin horns in position (x to x), pointing in towards the body and remembering which way they will face when body is turned right side out (see diagram page 3). Place the second body piece right side down on top and pin pieces together. Sew all around the body, securing the horns in place as you go, and leaving an opening for turning right side out and stuffing (as marked). Trim edges and clip around curves.

6 Sew foot pieces onto bottoms of legs. Turn body right side out.

7 Using a stuffing stick, push small amounts of stuffing into the arms and legs. Gradually fill the rest of the body until the stuffing is firm and even, but not too tight.

8 Hand sew the stuffing opening closed using a whip stitch.

{CONTINUED}

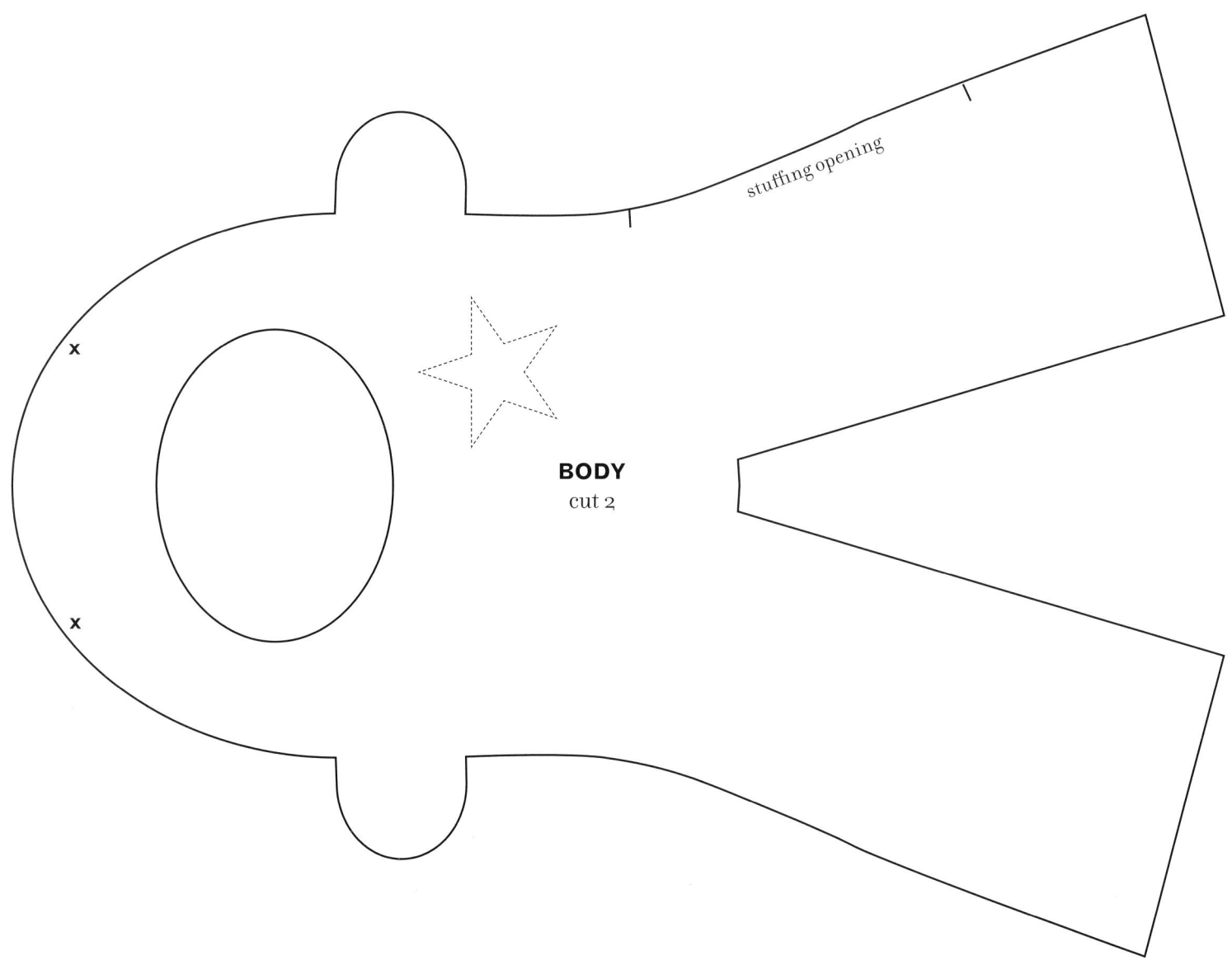

Enlarge template to 150% Seam allowance is included

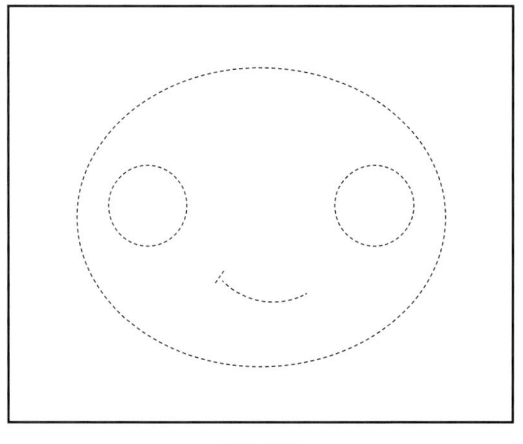

FACE
cut 1

STAR
cut 1

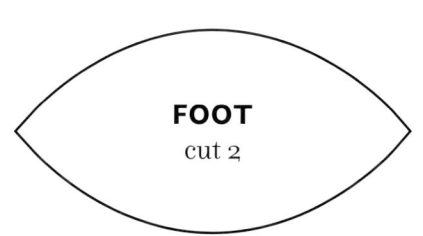

FOOT
cut 2

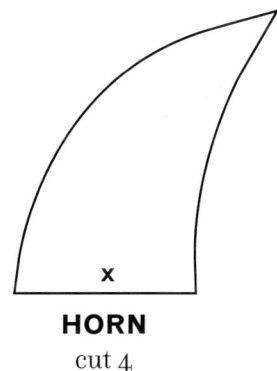

x

HORN
cut 4

cosmonaut devil

donkey

{My Little Mochi – mylittlemochi.typepad.com} MYRA MASUDA

To get the best results with this adorable donkey, use fabrics with a bit of stretch.

FINISHED SIZE
15 cm × 8 cm (6 in × 3 in) – excluding ears

TOOLS
- Iron
- Tracing paper
- Scissors
- Pins
- Sewing needle
- Sewing machine
- Stuffing stick (or chopstick or pencil)

MATERIALS
- Body fabric – an 18 cm × 30 cm (7 in × 12 in) piece of plain fabric for the main body; a 15 cm × 25 cm (6 in × 10 in) piece of new or vintage patterned fabric for the inner body.
- Extra fabric – a scrap of plain tan or cream fabric for the muzzle; scraps of white felt for the eyes and black felt for the pupils; interfacing for the ears.
- Thread – coloured sewing thread to match the body fabric; brown, pink and white embroidery thread for the face details, and black embroidery thread for the mane and tail.
- Stuffing – polyfill.

(CONTINUED)

{donkey}

INSTRUCTIONS

1 Trace and cut out the pattern using the template provided. Pin it to the fabric and cut out the pieces. You will need to cut 2 main body shapes, 2 inner body shapes, 6 ear shapes (2 in each fabric, plus 2 in interfacing), 2 muzzle shapes, 1 tail shape (cut on the bias), 2 eye shapes and 2 pupil shapes from your fabric.

2 Pin each muzzle piece to a main body piece, x to x, (right sides facing). Sew together.

3 Pin body/muzzle pieces together (right sides facing) and sew around the top of the body from A to B, leaving an opening for turning inside out and stuffing (as marked on the pattern).

4 Pin the inner body pieces together (right sides facing) and sew from A to B.

5 Pin the inner body piece to the main body piece (right sides facing), A to A and B to B. Sew together.

6 Trim edges and clip fabric around the curved edges. Be careful not to clip the seam. Turn right side out.

7 Using a stuffing stick, push small amounts of stuffing into the tight corners first – legs and muzzle. Gradually fill the rest of the body until the stuffing is firm and even, but not too tight.

8 Hand sew the stuffing opening closed using a ladder stitch.

9 For the eyes, sew each black felt oval onto a white felt circle and then position the eyes on the head as marked. Sew in place. Make a French knot with white embroidery thread for each pupil, as marked on the pattern. Use 3 strands of brown embroidery thread to sew the nostrils onto the muzzle using a straight stitch. Then use 3 strands of pink embroidery thread to sew the mouth using back stitch. Sew eyelashes with black embroidery thread.

10 For each ear, pin together a solid colour fabric piece, patterned fabric piece and interfacing (with fabrics right sides facing). Sew together, leaving the base open for turning right side out. Turn right side out and iron flat. Turn the base edge of the ears under 6 mm ($\frac{1}{4}$ in) and hand sew closed using a ladder stitch. Sew right and left bottom corners of the ear together to form a ring.

{donkey}

Position ears onto the head (y to y), and attach with a ladder stitch.

11 For the tail, fold the tail piece in half (rights sides facing) as marked on the pattern. Sew along the long edge to make a tube. Turn right side out. Turn the edges under 6 mm at each end and sew closed using a ladder stitch.

12 Use black embroidery thread for the end of the tail. Insert needle into tail, about 8 mm (⅓ in) from the end. Pull through, leaving about a 6 cm (2 in) tail. Cut off, leaving a tail of equal length. Repeat all the way around the end of the tail. Tie a piece of thread around the tail tassel, close to the end where it is attached to the tail. Attach the tie to the end of the tail so it won't slip off. Trim the tassel to a uniform length.

13 Pin finished tail to the back of the donkey at B. Attach with ladder stitch.

14 Use black embroidery thread to stitch the mane. Starting at point C, insert needle on right side of 'spine' and bring out 3 mm (⅛ in) over, on the left side of the spine, leaving about a 2.5 cm (1 in) tail on the right side. Insert needle at the first point of entry and bring out at the second point (effectively 'tying' the thread to the spine). Cut off, leaving a 2.5 cm (1 in) tail on the left side. Repeat this process until you've worked your way from point C to point D. Once finished, trim mane to a uniform length of about 2 cm (¾ in).

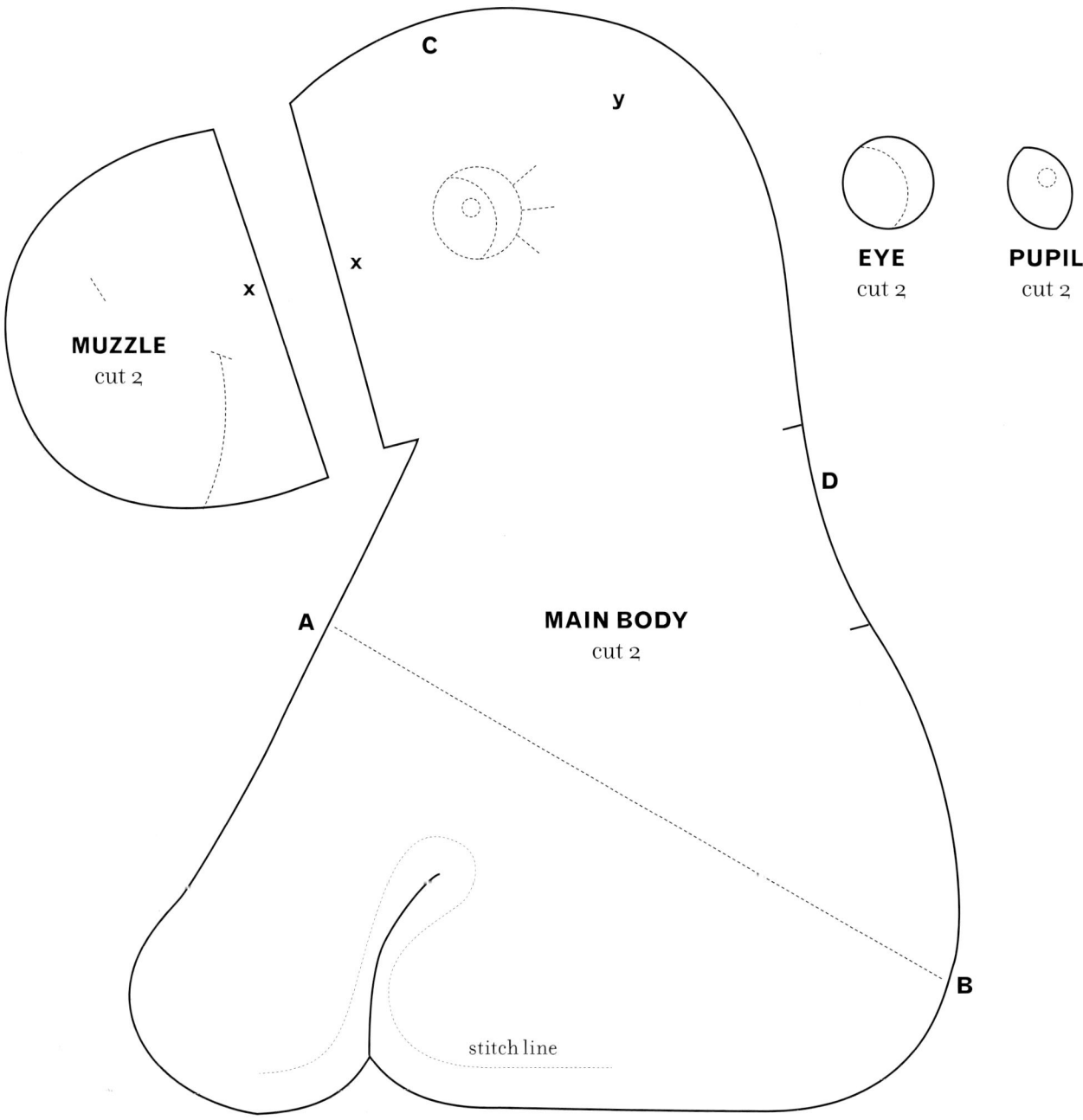

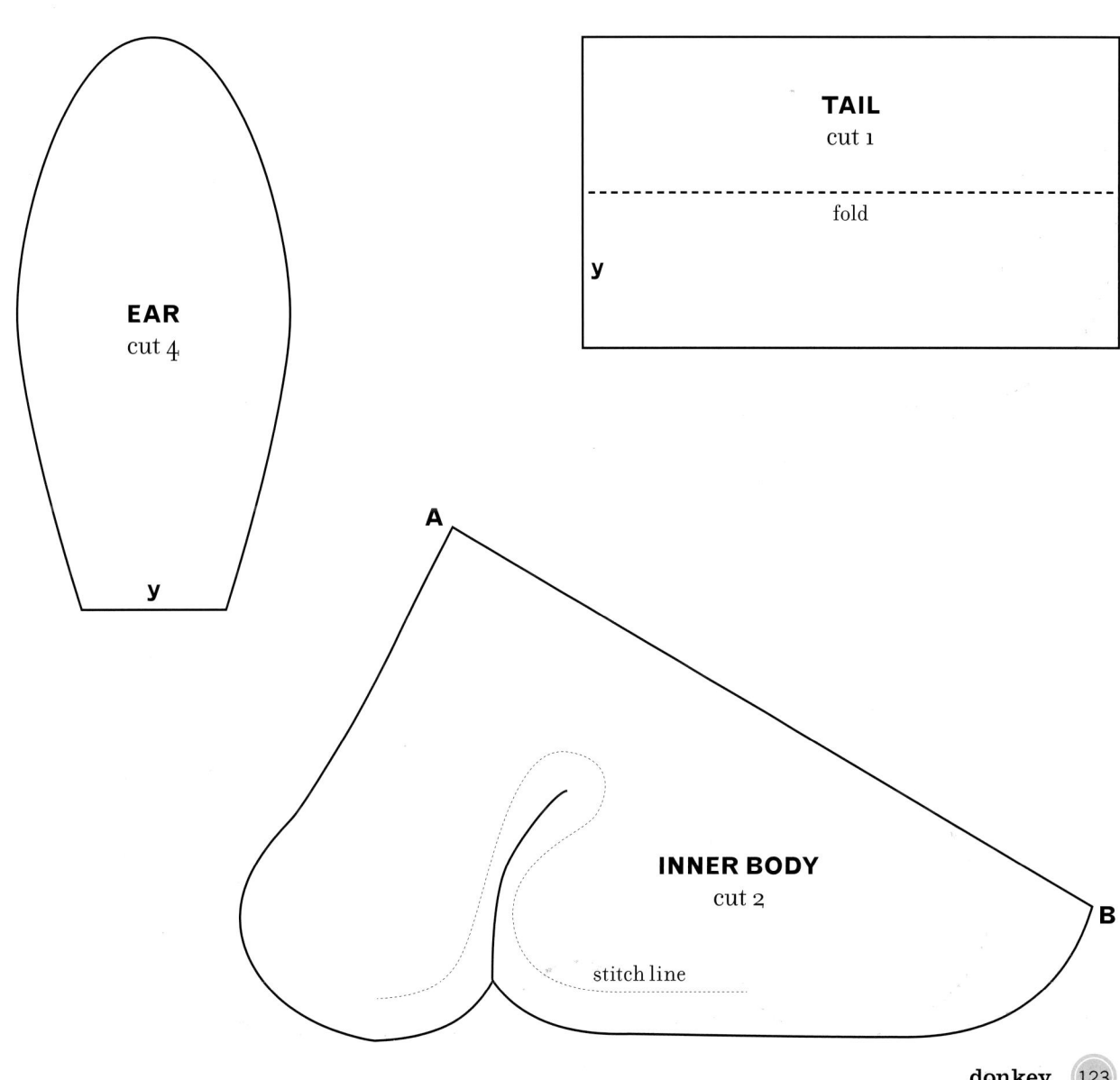

albert monkey

{www.hopskipjump.typepad.com} FIONA DALTON

This dapper gentleman can be made from recycled woolen clothing, and is a durable and dependable companion.

FINISHED SIZE
36 cm × 14 cm (14 in × 5½ in) – excluding arms

TOOLS
- Tracing paper
- Scissors
- Pins
- Sewing needle
- Sewing machine
- Stuffing stick (or chopstick or pencil)
- Iron

MATERIALS
- Body fabric – a 48 cm × 40 cm (19 in × 16 in) piece of sturdy woven wool or wool-blend fabric for the body (e.g. an old suit, blanket or flannel).
- Extra fabric – a 10 cm × 10 cm (4 in × 4 in) piece of felt in a contrasting colour for the face.
- Thread – coloured sewing thread to match woollen fabric, and embroidery thread of a contrasting colour to the felt.
- Decorations – two 10 mm (⅖ in) toy eyes (with washers).
- Stuffing – polyfill.

(CONTINUED)

{albert monkey}

INSTRUCTIONS

1 Trace and cut out the enlarged pattern using the template provided. Pin it to the appropriate fabric and cut out the pieces. You will need to cut 2 body shapes, 4 leg shapes, 4 arm shapes, 4 ear shapes, 1 mouth shape, 1 head (front) shape, 1 head (back) shape, and 1 eye shape.

2 For each arm, pin 2 pieces together (right sides facing), and sew, leaving the end open. Sew a straight stitch first, then a second line of zigzag stitch to secure. Leave a small opening as marked on the pattern, for turning right side out and stuffing. Repeat for the legs. For each ear, pin 2 pieces together (right sides facing), and sew, leaving the straight edge open. Turn legs, arms and ears right side out.

3 Place one of the body pieces right side up on your work surface. Pin the arms and legs in position (x to x and y to y), pointing in towards the body and remembering which way they will face when the body is turned right side out (see diagram page 3). Make sure the stuffing openings in the limbs end up on the underside of the arms and the inside of the legs (so they show the least). Place the second body piece right side down on top and pin the two body pieces together. Sew

{albert monkey}

using a straight stitch, securing the arms and legs in place as you go. Leave the hole at the neck open. Use a zigzag stitch to go around a second time for extra strength. After sewing, clip all curves close to the stitch line. Turn right side out.

4 Using a stuffing stick, push small amounts of stuffing into the arms and legs through the small openings until firmly stuffed. Hand stitch the stuffing openings closed (leaving the hole between the shoulders open). Stuff the body through the neck hole, but don't sew up the opening yet.

5 Take the fabric piece for the head front, and use a straight stitch to sew together the v-shape at the top.

6 Take the felt mouth and eye pieces and machine stitch these into place on the head front (see photo). Then make two holes through both the felt and the wool for the eyes and secure them with the washer. Use embroidery thread to cross-stitch a little X for the mouth.

7 Place the monkey head (front) right side up on your work surface. Pin the ears in position (z to z) pointing in towards the body. Place the head (back) fabric piece right side down on top. Sew a straight stitch, followed by a zigzag, to join the two head pieces together, leaving an opening at the base of the neck for stuffing. Turn right side out. Use a stuffing stick to firmly stuff the head.

8 Take the head and place the neck inside the hole between the shoulders, tucking it down inside the opening so that no raw edges are showing. Adjust the neck length until you are happy with how it looks, then pin it and hand sew around the base of the neck using a whip stitch.

9 You can dress your monkey in a pair of trousers or overalls (see instructions on page 128).

(CONTINUED)

{albert monkey}

Trousers

MATERIALS
- Fabric – a 30 cm × 38 cm (12 in × 15 in) piece of vintage or modern tweed, denim or heavy cotton.
- Thread – sewing thread to match the fabric.
- Decorations – trim, buttons or buckles for trousers (optional).

INSTRUCTIONS

1 Note that the pattern provided may require some adjustment for both width and length, depending on the type of fabric used for the monkey, and how much it has stretched once stuffed. If your fabric has stretched a lot once stuffed, remember to cut the trouser pieces wider to allow for the extra girth.

2 To make the trousers, trace and cut out the enlarged pattern using the template provided. Pin it to the fabric and cut out the pieces. You will need 4 trouser shapes.

3 Pin 2 of the pieces together (right sides facing) and sew a straight stitch from A to B. Repeat with the 2 remaining pieces. Open each piece out and iron the seams flat. Pin these 2 trouser pieces together (right sides facing) and sew a seam from C to D on each side.

4 Check trousers for fit and make any adjustments to length and waist as necessary. Hem the top raw edge of the trousers for the waistband. Sew an inner leg seam from B to E on each side. Trim and hem the bottom of each leg. Trim or extra material can be attached as braces, and buttons or buckles added as you desire.

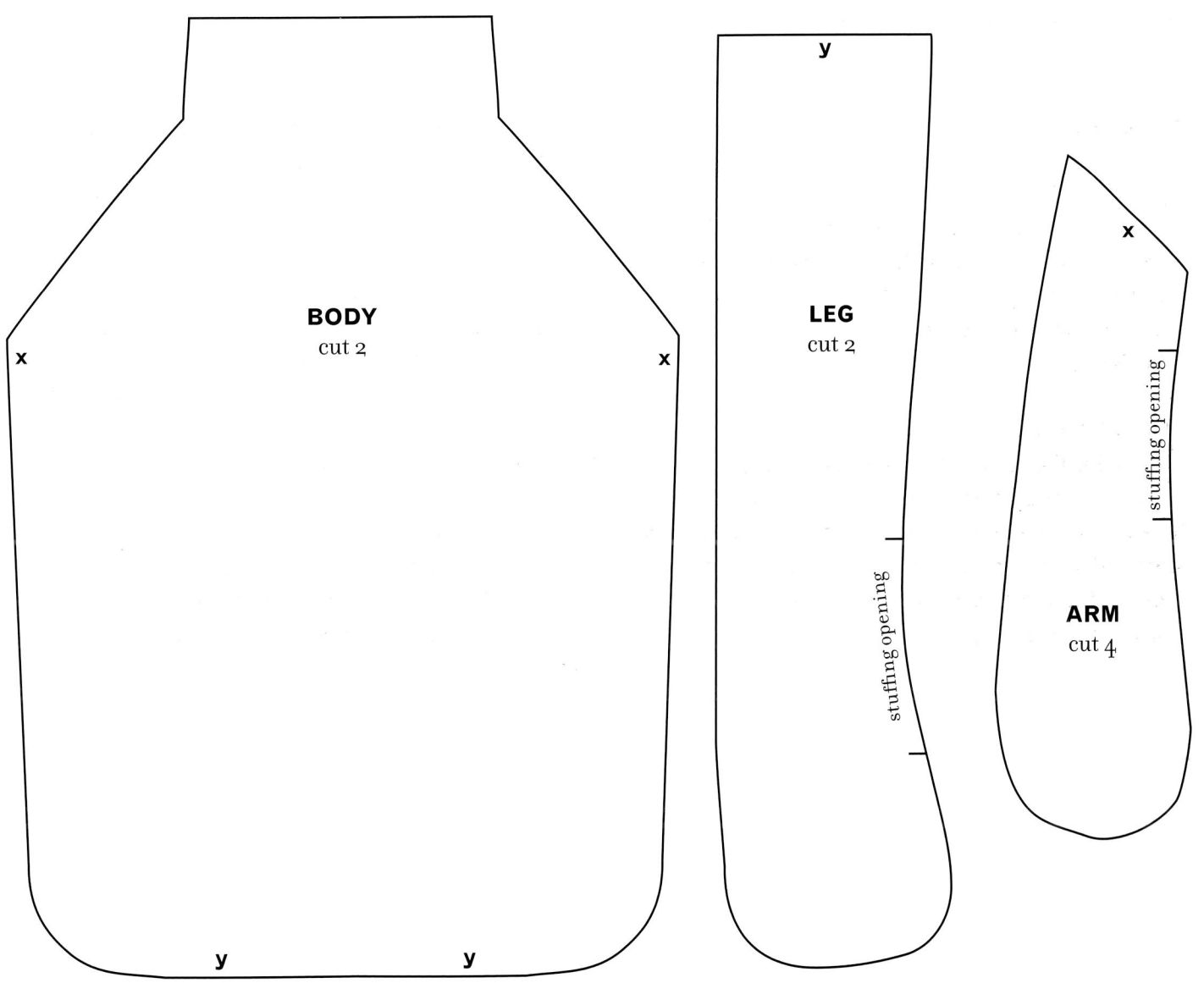

Enlarge template to 125% Seam allowance is included

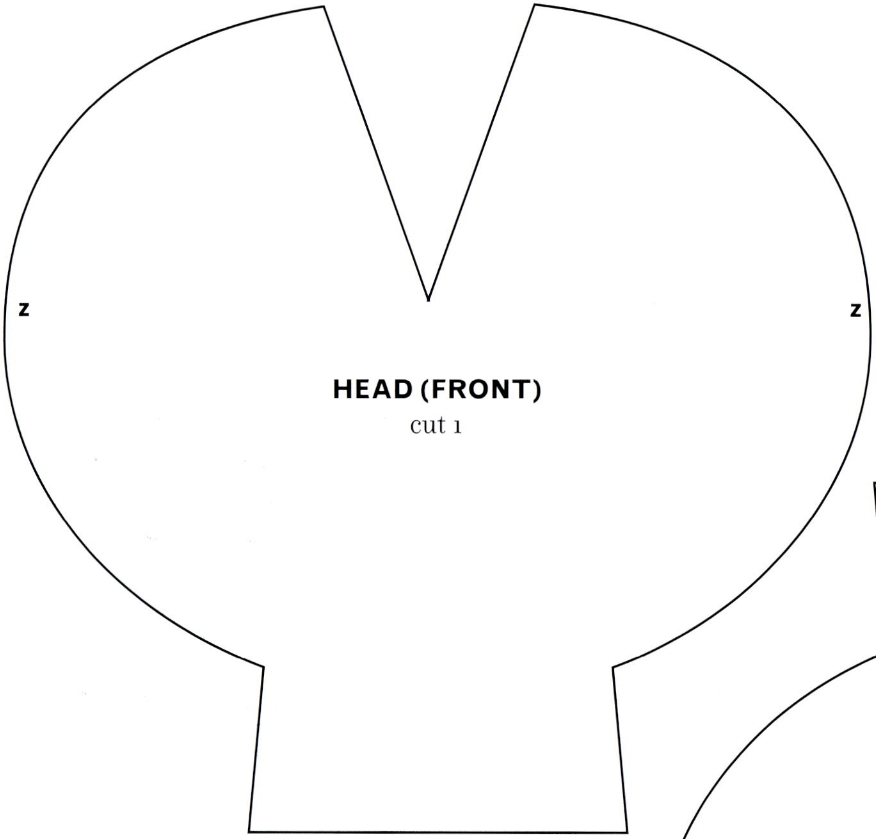

z   z

HEAD (FRONT)
cut 1

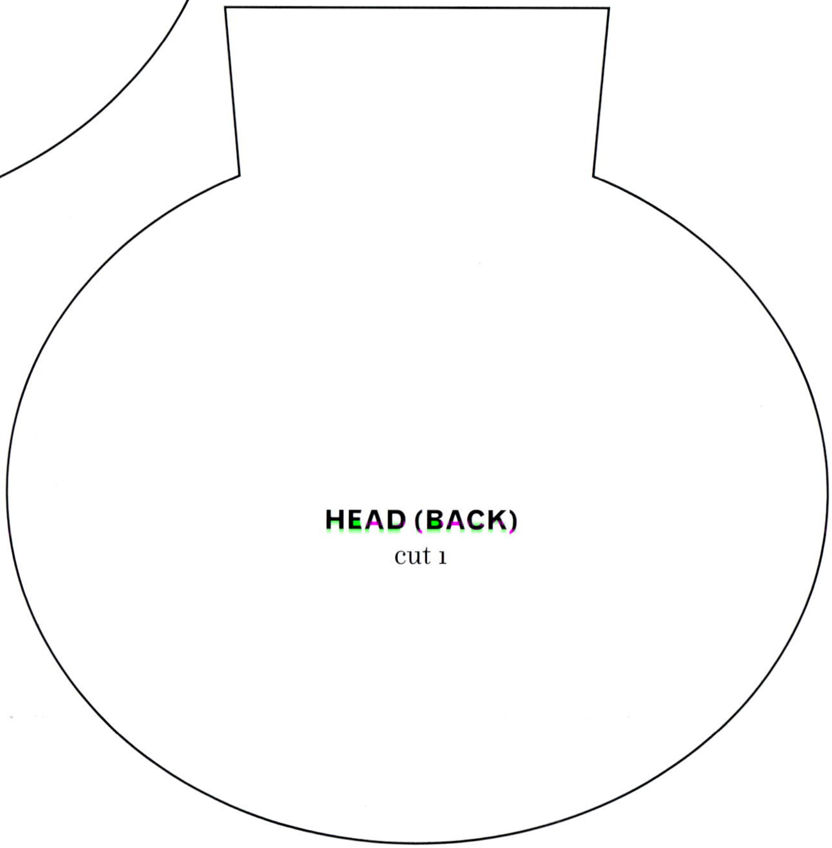

HEAD (BACK)
cut 1

130 albert monkey

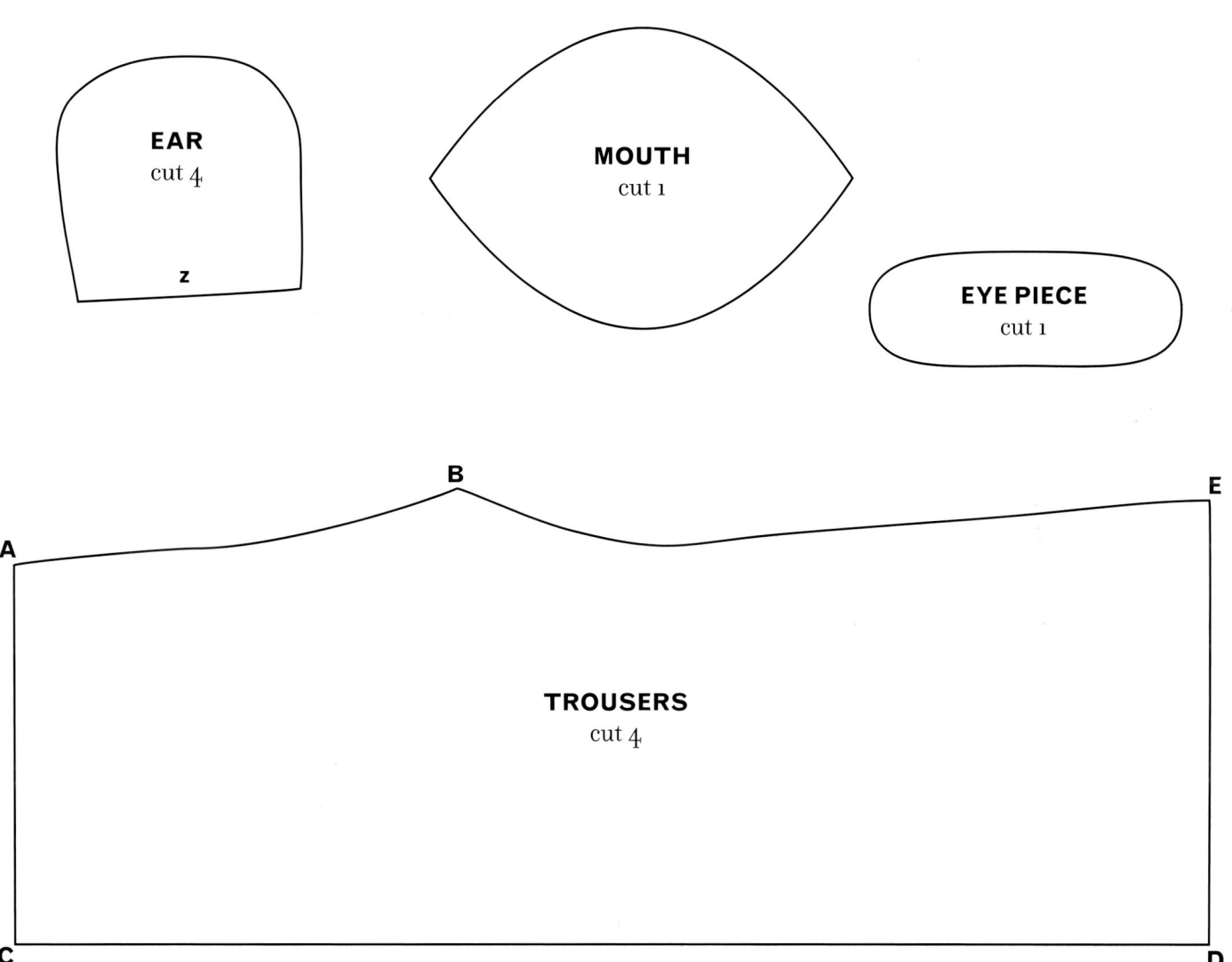

owl

{while she naps – www.whileshenaps.typepad.com} ABIGAIL PATNER GLASSENBERG

This wise old owl is almost like a small pillow. It has no small parts and therefore is safe for a baby. Because it is stuffed very firmly, this toy is best sewn on a sewing machine, with the machine set to a very small stitch length.

FINISHED SIZE
16 cm × 17 cm (6 in × 6½ in)

TOOLS
- Iron
- Tracing paper
- Scissors
- Pins
- Sewing needle
- Sewing machine
- Stuffing stick (or chopstick or pencil)
- Hole puncher (optional, but makes neat circles for pupils)

MATERIALS
- Body fabric – scraps of four coordinating fabrics: a light-coloured plain fabric for the upper body right and upper body left; another light-coloured fabric for the bottom and inner ears; a patterned fabric for the lower body and outer ears; a dark-coloured plain fabric for the sides and back.
- Extra fabric – scraps of light- and dark-coloured felt for the eyes and beak.
- Thread – coloured sewing thread to match the body fabric and to match the eye and beak felt.
- Stuffing – wool rovings or polyfill.

(CONTINUED)

{owl}

INSTRUCTIONS

1 Trace and cut out the enlarged pattern using the template provided. Pin it to the fabric and cut out the pieces. You will need to cut 1 upper body left shape, 1 upper body right shape, 1 lower body shape, 1 side shape (cut on the fold), 1 bottom shape, 1 back shape, 4 eye shapes (2 in dark felt, 2 in light felt), 4 ear shapes (2 in the light fabric used for the bottom, 2 in the patterned fabric used for the lower body) and 1 beak shape.

2 Pin together upper body left and upper body right pieces (right sides facing), and sew from A to B. Open out and iron the seam to one side. Pin lower body to upper body (right sides facing) and sew from B to C1, then from B to C2. (Don't worry if the stitches at B are not perfect because B will be covered at the end by the owl's beak.) Trim edges and clip fabric around the curves. Be careful not to clip the seam. Iron seam to one side.

3 For each ear, pin outer ear piece (light fabric) to inner ear piece (patterned fabric) (right sides facing) and sew, leaving an opening at the base for turning right side out. Trim edges and turn right side out. Iron. Fold the left and right sides into the centre (see photo) and iron to crease. Use a ladder stitch to sew the left side to the right side, about a quarter of the way up the fold.

4 Place the body piece right side up on your work surface. Pin the ears in position (x to x), pointing in towards the body (see diagram on page 3).

5 Pin the side piece to the front body piece (right sides facing), D1 to D1 and A to A, and sew from A to D1, then from A to D2, sewing over the base of the ears to secure them as you go.

6 Pin back piece to side piece (right sides together), E to E, and sew from E to F1, then from E to F2. Trim edges and clip around curves.

{owl}

7 Pin bottom piece to front pieces (D1 to D1 and D2 to D2), right sides facing, and sew. Sew bottom to sides and back, leaving an opening for turning right side out and stuffing (as marked on the pattern).

8 Check seams for strength, then trim and clip curves. Carefully turn right side out, pulling ears and top of head out first.

9 Using a stuffing stick, stuff owl firmly, moulding the sides so there are no lumps and shaping the bottom so that it's flat and the owl can stand on its own.

10 Hand sew the stuffing opening closed using a ladder stitch.

11 For the eyes, use a hole puncher to punch a hole in the centre of each light-coloured piece of felt, as marked on the pattern. Attach each piece of light felt to a piece of dark felt using double-sided iron-on adhesive, or with small stitches. Position eyes on finished owl and sew into place with small stitches.

12 Sew beak into place (at B) with small stitches.

Englarge template to 140% Seam allowance is included

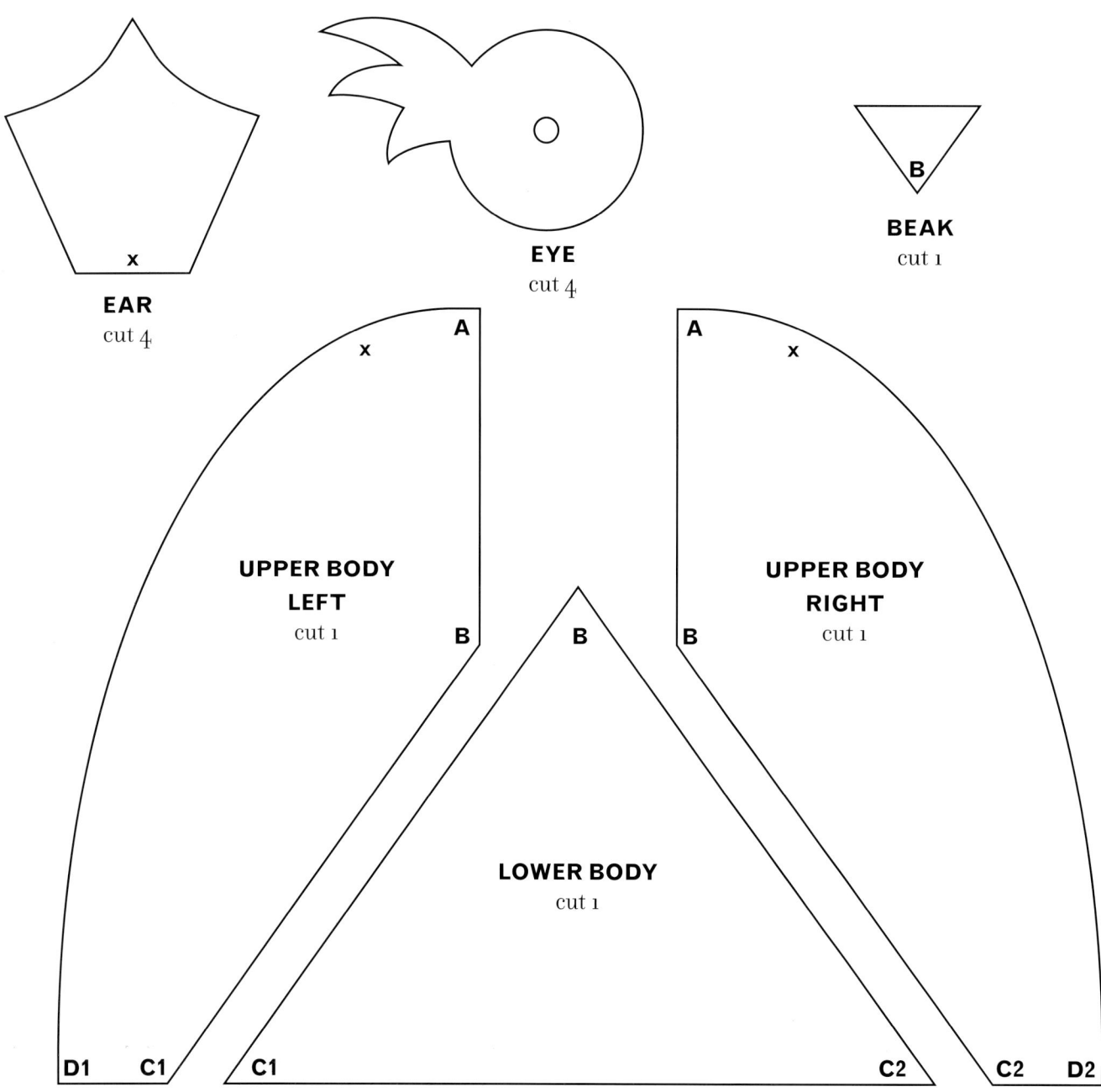

136 owl

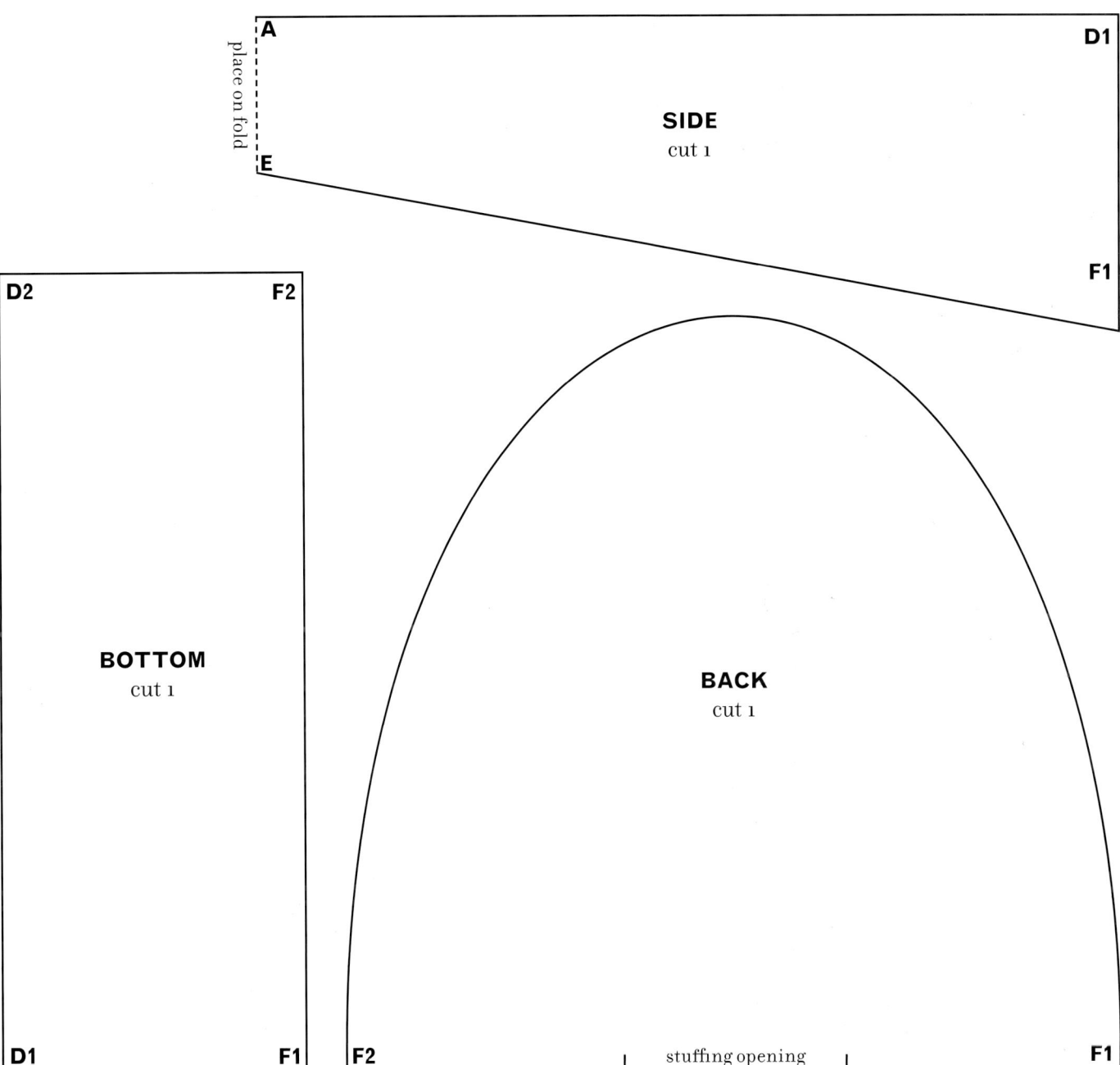

owl 137

glossary

Back stitch Work from right to left. Pass needle up from underside of fabric, then insert it about 3 mm to the right of this point. Bring needle up again about 3 mm to the left of the starting point. Continue in this manner.

Basting The action of sewing large removable stitches by hand or machine, in order to hold fabrics in place before sewing securely. To baste two pieces of fabric together by hand, make a series of very large running stitches along the seam line, taking several stitches on your needle before pulling the thread through. Secure with two back stitches close together. Once you've decided that the seam is appropriate, stitch the fabric permanently, then carefully unpick the back stitches and remove the basting thread.

CC Contrast colour.

Chain stitch (ch) Yarn over hook, then pull yarn through stitch on hook.

Clipping the seam allowance Curved seams should be clipped so that they will be smooth when turned right side out and stuffed. After sewing, trim edges, but leave at least a 10 mm border. With scissors, nick fabric around the curved edges (tight curves will need more nicks). Be careful to not clip the seam. Outer curves should be 'notched', whereby you clip a small triangle out of the seam allowance.

Cut on the bias Cut the fabric at a 45 degree angle across the warp and weft threads.

Cut on the fold Fold your fabric in half before cutting out the piece from the pattern, with the folded line positioned as marked on the pattern. You will end up with a pattern piece of double thickness, joined down one side by the fold.

Double crochet (dc) Insert hook into next stitch, then yarn over hook. Pull yarn through stitch (so there's 2 loops on the hook), then yarn over hook and pull yarn through both loops on hook.

Fat quarter A fabric measurement equivalent to a quarter of a yard (27 cm); a common measurement that all fabric shops will be familiar with.

French knot Pass needle up from underside of fabric, at the point where the knot is to lie. Wrap the thread around the needle several times, then insert needle very

{glossary}

close to where it came up. Pull tight to secure.

Half treble crochet (htr) Yarn over hook, then insert hook into next stitch. Pull yarn through stitch (so there's 3 loops on the hook), then yarn over hook and pull yarn through all 3 loops on hook.

Knit stitch Insert right needle through front of the first stitch on the left needle. Wrap yarn around tip of right needle, then use the right needle to draw yarn through the stitch on the left needle. Slip original stitch off the left needle. Continue in this manner.

Ladder stitch Line up fabrics to be joined side by side. Pass needle up from underside of first fabric, then insert parallel into second fabric. Bring needle up again about 3 mm along on the second fabric. Insert needle parallel into first fabric. Continue in this manner. (The stitches should be almost invisible.)

MC Main colour.

Ric rac A type of ribbon.

Right sides facing When sewing, you place pieces of fabric with their 'pretty' sides facing each other (i.e. the sides that will eventually face out). You sew on the 'wrong' side of the fabric so that the seams will be hidden when the piece is turned right side out.

Running stitch Push the needle in and out of the fabric in a straight line, along the edge of the seam. Make stitches on the top of equal length, and stitches on the underside also of equal length, but about half as long as the stitches on the top.

Satin stitch Use consecutive straight stitches, very close together, across the entire shape to be filled.

Slip stitch (sewing) Work from right to left. This stitch is used to join folded edges of fabric. Pass needle up through folded edge of first piece of fabric, then pick up a few threads from the folded edge of the second piece of fabric. Pick up a few threads on the first piece. Continue in this manner. (The stitches should be almost invisible.)

Slip stitch (sl st) (crochet) Insert hook into next stitch, then yarn over hook and pull yarn through both loops on hook.

{glossary}

Split stitch Work from left to right. Pass needle up from underside of fabric, then make a small back stitch to the right, passing the needle up between the two plies of working thread. Continue in this manner.

Stem stitch Work from left to right. Pass needle up from underside of fabric to the left of the working line, then insert it about 6 mm to the right on the other side of the working line. Bring it up again on the other side of the line, about 3 mm to the right of your starting point. Continue in this manner.

Straight stitch Single spaced stitches.

Stretch stitch Set your sewing machine to stretch stitch (if it doesn't have a stretch stitch, use zigzag).

Treble crochet (tr) Yarn over hook, then insert hook into next stitch. Pull yarn through stitch (so there are 3 loops on the hook), then yarn over hook and pull yarn through 2 loops on hook. Yarn over hook and pull yarn through 2 loops on hook again.

Turning chain Turn the work so your hook is at the beginning of the next row. Crochet one or more chain stitches, as specified in the pattern.

Whip stitch Work from right to left. Pass needle up from underside of first piece of fabric, then insert needle a little to the left on the second piece of fabric to make a diagonal stitch. Bring needle up parallel on the first piece of fabric. Continue in this manner. (Stitches should be as small as possible.)

Thanks — to the incredibly talented crafters from around the globe who have contributed their stunning work to this book.

fabric credits

Every effort has been made to trace and acknowledge fabric designers and manufacturers. The publisher would be pleased to hear from any copyright holders who have not been acknowledged.

Polly
The orange spotted fabric on the arms is 'Everything but the Kitchen Sink' by RJR Fabrics. The striped fabric used for the legs is 'NS-01 Narrow Stripe' by Kaffe Fassett. Other fabrics are vintage.

Bunny
Yarn is all thrifted (second-hand). Felt is from Panduro Hobby (www.pandurohobby.com).

Plurbit
The face fabric for the brown Plurbit is a from a vintage necktie.

Henny House
The roof fabric is 'D1417-265' from the 'Flea Market Fancy' collection by Denyse Schmidt for Free Spirit. The leg, arm and back fabric is 'D1414-402' from the same collection.

Guardian Angel
The body fabric is corduroy, 'Babyroy Big Oli Flower – Chilly Pepper' by BBG/BizzKids.

Hector Giraffe
The spotted fabric is by Kei Fabrics. The middle body fabric is by Amy Butler for Rowan Fabrics. The upper and lower body fabric is by Valorie Wells for Free Spirit Fabrics. The plain brown fabric is from Spotlight. The wool felt is from Winterwood Toys (www.winterwoodtoys.com).

Mamma Bear
The small spotted/checked fabric on the apron is '148 Vintage Flower Garden' by Maywood Studio. The large blue spotted fabric on the apron and hands is 'D#5743' by Robert Kaufman. Other fabrics are vintage.

Kangaroo
The spotted fabric is 'Hot Dot' by Alexander Henry Fabrics.

Blossom Bunny
The patterned fabric is a 1930s reproduction fabric, 'Granny's Twelve' by Darlene Zimmerman for Chanteclaire Fabrics.

Beetle Bug
All vintage fabrics.

Cat
Vintage fabrics.

Donkey
The spotted fabric is 'Aunt Grace Tenth Anniversary 2001–02' by Judie Rothermel for Marcus Brothers Textiles, Inc.

Albert Monkey
The trousers are vintage wool tweed.

Owl
The floral fabric on the lower body and ears is 'D1410-018' from the 'Flea Market Fancy' collection by Denyse Schmidt for Free Spirit.

VIKING

Published by the Penguin Group
Penguin Group (Australia)
250 Camberwell Road, Camberwell, Victoria 3124, Australia
(a division of Pearson Australia Group Pty Ltd)
Penguin Group (USA) Inc.
375 Hudson Street, New York, New York 10014, USA
Penguin Group (Canada)
90 Eglinton Avenue East, Suite 700, Toronto ON M4P 2Y3, Canada
(a division of Pearson Penguin Canada Inc.)
Penguin Books Ltd
80 Strand, London WC2R 0RL, England
Penguin Ireland
25 St Stephen's Green, Dublin 2, Ireland
(a division of Penguin Books Ltd)
Penguin Books India Pvt Ltd
11 Community Centre, Panchsheel Park, New Delhi – 110 017, India
Penguin Group (NZ)
67 Apollo Drive, Rosedale, North Shore 0632, New Zealand
(a division of Pearson New Zealand Ltd)
Penguin Books (South Africa) (Pty) Ltd
24 Sturdee Avenue, Rosebank, Johannesburg 2196, South Africa

Penguin Books Ltd, Registered Offices: 80 Strand, London, WC2R 0RL, England

First published by Penguin Group (Australia), 2007

10 9 8 7 6

Text copyright © Penguin Group (Australia)
Design and photographs copyright © Penguin Group (Australia) 2007
Copyright © of individual doll designs remains with the creators
Patterns are intended for personal use only.

All rights reserved. Without limiting the rights under copyright reserved above,
no part of this publication may be reproduced, stored in or introduced into a retrieval
system, or transmitted, in any form or by any means (electronic, mechanical, photocopying,
recording or otherwise), without the prior written permission of both the copyright owner
and the above publisher of this book.

Design by Claire Tice © Penguin Group (Australia)
Photography by Julie Renouf
Typeset by Post Pre-press Group, Brisbane, Queensland
Colour reproduction by Splitting Image, Clayton, Victoria
Printed in China by 1010 Printing International Ltd

National Library of Australia
Cataloguing-in-Publication data:

Softies.
ISBN 978 0 670 07082 4 (pbk.).
1. Dollmaking. 2. Soft toys.

745.59221

penguin.com.au